Lescudjack Hill
Lescudjack Castle
Three Tuns Hotel
Lannoweth House
Battery
Station
Goods Shed
Stone Yard
Hotel
Meth. Chapel (Prim.)
Albert Street
High Water Mark of Ordinary Tides
Chyandour Cliff
Mooring Posts
Gas Works
Gridiron
Iron Foundry
Iron Foundry
Store
HARBOUR
Limekiln
PENZANCE
Lighthouse
Mooring Posts
Dry Dock
Capstan

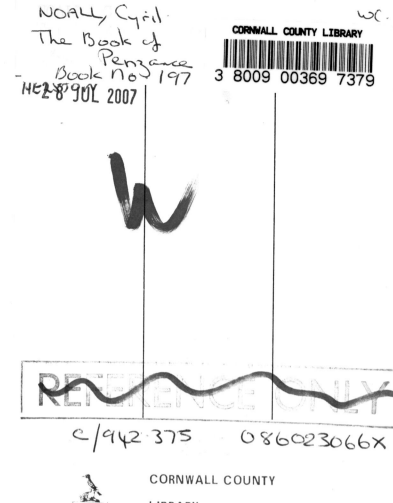

The Book of Penzance 1983
has been published as a Limited
Edition of which this is

Number 197

A complete list of the
original subscribers is printed
at the back of the book

THE BOOK OF PENZANCE

Map of Mount's Bay, c1515. (BM)

Penzance from the Sea

THE BOOK OF PENZANCE

BY

CYRIL NOALL

With additional material on
Newlyn, Marazion & St Michael's Mount
By DOUGLAS WILLIAMS

Photographic Adviser
WILLIAM THOMAS

BARRACUDA BOOKS LIMITED
BUCKINGHAM, ENGLAND
MCMLXXXIII

PUBLISHED BY BARRACUDA BOOKS LIMITED
BUCKINGHAM, ENGLAND
AND PRINTED BY
HOLYWELL PRESS LIMITED
OXFORD, ENGLAND

BOUND BY
GREEN STREET BINDERY LIMITED
OXFORD, ENGLAND

JACKET PRINTED BY
CHENEY & SONS LIMITED
BANBURY, OXON

LITHOGRAPHY BY
SOUTH MIDLANDS LITHOPLATES LIMITED
LUTON, ENGLAND

DISPLAY SET IN BASKERVILLE
& TEXT SET IN 10/11 pt BASKERVILLE BY
KEY COMPOSITION
NORTHAMPTON, ENGLAND

ISBN 0 86023 066 X

Contents

Acknowledgements

We wish to express our grateful thanks to William Thomas, of Carbis Bay, for his careful and painstaking work with the photographs used in this book, nearly all of which were specially taken or copied by him. Acknowledgements are also made to the following: Adrianne Buckley, of the British Library Map Library; staff of the National Portrait Gallery, London; S. C. McMenamin, Assistant Keeper, Department of Manuscripts, British Library; M. Frankel, Public Record Office, London; Penzance Town Council, and their Clerk, W. J. Williams, for permission to use the records of the former Penzance Borough Council and photographs at Penlee House Museum; Irene Traill, Curator, Penlee House Museum; Terry Knight, Cornwall County Library Local Studies Department, Redruth; P. L. Hull, Archivist, and staff of the County Record Office, Truro; H. L. Douch, Curator, and R. D. Penhallurick, County Museum, Truro; John Farmer, Cornwall County Librarian; staff of the Penzance Branch, Cornwall County Library; Committee of the Penzance (Morrab Gardens) Library; A. Holman, of N. Holman & Sons, Ltd, Marine Engineers, Dry Dock, Wharf Road, Penzance; Canon W. R. Newton, Vicar of St Mary the Virgin, Penzance; Penwith District Council, for granting facilities at St John's Hall, Penzance; John Page, Editor, *The Cornishman*, Penzance. Mrs Pat Pilkerton, Sam Bennetts; Ted Ford; Andrew Besley; George Waterhouse; David and Roland Woods; the National Trust and the Marazion Town Trust and the Marazion Town Council for their permission to use photographs. For their assistance with the text: Ben Batten, Francis Hosking, Bill Baker, Kenneth Northey, Andrew Munson, John Corin and Mrs Jane Williams.

Foreword

by Councillor Mrs Margaret Beckerleg JP Town Mayor of Penzance

Penzance is today the centre of the Penwith peninsula in administration and in trade. It was not always so, but 'Pensans' down the centuries has played an important role along the Mount's Bay coastline.

This book traces that history from its earliest times to the present day, conveying to the readers at home and overseas the spirit of Cornish enterprise, and the splendid heritage that we so much treasure.

I hope the book will bring to all readers an appreciation of local traditions, and maintain the enthusiasm to ensure their survival, together with the continued development and prosperity of the area.

There is also – and always – a place in the Cornish heart for nostalgia, and this book with its many illustrations highlights those memories from the early years of photography.

It gives me great pleasure to welcome this *Book of Penzance,* combining as it does the stories of neighbouring Newlyn, Marazion and St Michael's Mount, particularly during my term of office as Town Mayor.

I congratulate the authors and publishers, thank all who have contributed to the book, and wish it well.

October 1983

Margaret Beckerleg.

Introduction

Had some mediaeval futurologist ventured to predict in, say, the early fourteenth century, that of the three small communities then bordering the western half of Mount's Bay – Marghasiewe (Marazion), Pensans (Penzance) and Mousehole – the only one ultimately destined to excel in size, population and influence was Pensans, his assertion must surely have been received with amused incredulity. It would have been pointed out to him that Marghasiewe, as the traditional reception centre for pilgrims visiting St Michael's Mount, possessed the advantages of a prestigious antiquity and flourishing fairs and markets, and that Mousehole boasted the largest number of fishing boats and people, while by contrast, Penzance ranked as a relatively insignificant fishing village with seemingly little potential for development.

Yet it was Penzance which gained the ascendancy. Mousehole dropped out of the running at a fairly early stage, being content to concentrate on its fishing interests. Marghasiewe, by winning a charter of incorporation from Elizabeth I in 1595, then appeared to take the lead; but in the intensifying struggle to become the principal market town in West Cornwall, Pensans, by employing rather forceful tactics, proved itself the victor, its triumph recognised in the grant of borough status by James I in 1614. Nothing, runs the old adage, succeeds like success, and its truth was well demonstrated when, in 1663, Penzance received a further Royal accolade as a coinage town from Charles II. From then on its progress was continual and assured, based on a steadily increasing seaborne trade, markets, fairs, fisheries and the tin coinage.

Just why should Penzance have prospered in this way, though endowed with no particular advantages by comparison with its neighbours? The answer must surely lie in the enterprising spirit of its inhabitants and their determination to win for themselves and their town a position of undisputed pre-eminence. An early demonstration of this was the speed with which they overcame the setback caused by the destructive Spanish raid in 1595, and it has played a decisive part in the town's progress ever since. During the last century it was particularly active in creating Penzance's excellent harbour, docks, promenade, public buildings and parks, and more recently has enabled the town to adapt so readily to its new role as the centre for local government in West Cornwall and as the hub of land, sea and air communications for a still wider area.

Whether as a place of permanent or temporary residence, modern Penzance has a great deal to offer. Its glorious setting, overlooking the sparkling waters of Mount's Bay, an equable climate which, nearly two centuries ago, established its reputation as a health resort, and the varied cultural, scholastic and commercial facilities available make it a marvellously self-sufficient town, where a full and satisfying life may be enjoyed in the midst of one of the most romantic and beautiful parts of the West country.

Penzance possesses much historic and architectural interest. At the western end of Market Jew Street may still be seen the old Star Inn, under whose long-vanished portico the youthful Humphry Davy entertained his friends with recitations, while out at Alverton stands the thatched farmhouse where another high-spirited local lad with a great destiny before him – Edward Boscawen, the future Lord Exmouth, hero of many sea fights with the French, and renowned for his reduction of the notorious slave city of Algiers in 1816 – once lived with his grandmother, the long-suffering Madam Woodhouse. And it was at another house, just below St Mary's vicarage in Chapel Street, that there dwelt a young girl called Maria Branwell who later, as the wife of Rev Patrick Brontë of Haworth parsonage in Yorkshire, became mother of the immortal Brontë sisters, Charlotte, Emily and Anne and their brother Branwell.

Charming Regency squares and terraces, much solid Victorian and Edwardian architecture in the business and older residential areas, quaint passageways and alleys near the harbour, and the remarkable kaleidoscope of buildings of many periods and styles to be found in Chapel Street, afford much of interest to the observant eye. Over all presides the tall tower of St Mary's Church, dominating the scene from the spot where Penzance began so many centuries ago, the 'holy headland' which gave the place its name.

In the following pages an attempt has been made to relate the story of the rise and development of the town from its earliest days to the present time both in words and, more especially, pictures. Although the camera did not come into general use until the mid-19th century, it was able to capture some aspects of a much older Penzance which have now passed away, besides recording many intriguing glimpses of the passing scene.

Through its lens is revealed a town of quite extraordinary quaintness and individuality belonging to a far more leisurely age than ours, when schooners and brigantines crowded its harbour, horse-drawn 'buses and wagons rattled through its streets, and gas lights twinkled at dusk in small-paned shop windows and along the granite pavements. To see this panorama of the past unfold is to gain a deeper appreciation of the manner in which Penzance has evolved into the prosperous, busy and yet eminently civilised place it is today.

Midsummer Eve in Dolly Pentreath's Day

Midsummer-eve to Dolly brought a treat,
When at Penzance, the Cornish world all meet;
The Bay is in a blaze; on every height
Behold a bonfire sheds its awful light;
And rockets from a thousand hands take flight,
And gambol in th' illuminated fields of air;
The stars, eclipsed, outnumbered, disappear;
While echoing shouts from every quarter rise,
And glad the ambient earth, and sea, and skies.
To close the scene, the joyful crowds advance,
And join their friendly hands in gay Penzance:
Rank, sex, or age makes no distinction here,
Th' amusement of the night their only care.
To "thread the needle," now their skill they try;
All, joined and rushing, shout "an eye! an eye!"
The hindmost stop, the foremost wheel about;
"An eye! an eye!" more loudly still they shout.
The eye is formed; the couple in the rear
Stand wide apart, their clasped hands in the air.
This arch, or eye, the foremost swift pass through,
And all the living thread behind them draw.
The following is the feast day of St. John,
When all the world their best attire put on;
Boats, barges, smacks, and sloops crowd round the shore,
And all is jollity and gay uproar.
All rush on board and launch into the Bay,
While music cheers them on their watery way.
Meanwhile upon the land a fair is seen,
And sturdy wrestlers on the joyful green;
Where many a "Cornish hug" and many a fall,
Loud plaudits from the pleased spectators call.
More of this ancient sport I might rehearse
Had not great Homer put it into verse:
Midnight, at length, her peaceful curtain draws,
And Pleasure yields her empire to Repose.

(By 'A Cornubian', in *Recreations in Rhyme,* 1834.)

Early Years

Penzance, today the principal town and seaport of the Penwith Hundred of Cornwall, originated from a tiny community of fisherfolk, who kept their boats within the shelter of the small headland terminating at the Battery Rocks, which marks the southern boundary of the present harbour. Upon this headland was erected, probably in the twelfth century, a little chapel dedicated to St Anthony, the patron saint of fishermen. The chapel formed a prominent landmark visible for some miles around, and gave rise to the Celtic place name of *Pen Sans*, holy headland (from *Pen*, head, and *Sans*, holy) by which, in a slightly modified form, the town is known to this day. In after years, when its true meaning had been forgotten, the name was re-interpreted to mean 'head of the sands', 'head of the channel', or 'Saint's head', this last resulting in the gruesome device of St John the Baptist's head on a charger being chosen as the town's arms.

In early times, before any human settlement, the site must have been different for considerable coast erosion has since taken place. The well known 'submerged forest' of Mount's Bay affords the clearest proof of the sea's encroachment. From Newlyn to the Wherry Rocks and from Chyandour to Marazion River severe storms combined with low tides have frequently exposed its remains. Just east of the rocks lying offshore from Chyandour, Joseph Carne during the early part of the last century found a number of tree trunks, mostly entire, lying prostrate in every direction, almost level with the surface of the sandy beach. Some measured 20 feet long with diameters of from twelve to six inches; the bark and wood, for more than an inch deep, were usually decayed, but the inside was hard, though porous, and quite black; those which he examined proved to be oak. Fifty yards further east branches of hazel and birch were found. When the *Zephyr* was wrecked on the eastern beach around the year 1833, her hull forced from the sand the trunk of an enormous oak, to which the bark still clung in a state of excellent preservation. Sir Gavin de Beer radio-carbon dated samples taken from the forest to around 1700 BC. It has been conjectured that St Michael's Mount may have been encompassed by this forest, but its supposed Celtic name of *Karrik Luz en Kuz*, the

Hoar Rock in the Wood, seems to have been 'borrowed' from the strikingly similar Mont St Michel in Normandy.

The history of Penzance during Neolithic and Bronze Age times is virtually a blank; but in Lescudjack Castle it possesses a large and impressive Iron Age earthwork, occupying a commanding position on top of a hill overlooking the eastern entrance of the town. Unhappily, it has not been well preserved. Courtney lamented in 1845 that only a part of the circle then remained – 'and this is in such condition that antiquarian eyes alone can find any thing of interest therein'. It has suffered further deterioration since, and is probably now beyond restoration. There is a smaller, but far more perfect, earthwork on the western side of Penzance, known as Lesingey Round, and some slight remains of a third at Tolcarne, Newlyn.

Although the Romans conquered Cornwall, they exercised only minimal control there, being interested mainly in trading with the natives for tin. This tin trade had been established several centuries before their arrival by merchants from Greek settlements in the Mediterranean. The metal, cast in ingots shaped like *astragali* (ankle bones) was taken in wagons to the tidal island of Ictis (St Michael's Mount) where it was purchased by the merchants, shipped to Gaul, and transported on horseback to the mouth of the Rhone. Diodorus, a Sicilian historian of the 1st century AD, flatteringly described the inhabitants of Belerium (Penwith) as being 'very fond of strangers and from their intercourse with foreign merchants are civilised in their manner of life'.

Christianity was established in Cornwall during the fifth century largely through the efforts of Irish, Welsh and Breton missionaries, who bestowed their names as well as their religion on many towns and parishes throughout the county. Unfortunately, no evidence has survived of any Christian presence at Penzance until the 10th century, to which period may be assigned the rather splendid Celtic cross which, after a peripatetic career, now reposes in Penlee Park. Its original site is not known, but when first recorded in the early part of last century, it stood in the Bullock Market (now the Greenmarket) and was used by farmers as a tethering post for their pigs. Getting in the way of traffic, it was then moved to the bottom of Causewayhead. On being dug up for this purpose an inscription was found near its base which Rev C. V. Le Grice deciphered as *Hic Procumbant Corpora Piorum.* From Causewayhead it was transferred to the western end of the Market House, then to the Morrab Gardens, and finally to Penlee. Another inscription discovered on the side of the cross by Prof Macalister was read by him as *Regis Ricati Crux,* 'the cross of King Ricatus'.

It is tempting to speculate that Ricatus may have been the last of the independent local monarchs who held sway before the Saxon subjugation of Cornwall by Athelstan in AD 926. The Saxon conquest effectively brought to an end the ancient Celtic church there, and Athelstan gave a clear indication of the new order of things in matters religious, by establishing a College of Priests at St Buryan in place of the former Celtic foundation.

We owe our earliest surviving documentary record to the Domesday survey of 1086. William, who had himself been a vassal, knew how easy it was for vassals to rebel against their king, and he accordingly arranged that there should be no great feudatory lords in England, except those holding estates in Cornwall, the Welsh Marches and on the northern frontier, the three districts that formed the barriers between the conquered Anglo-Saxons and the still unsubdued Celts.

Cornwall, with the exception of some monastic and church property, was given entirely to Robert, Earl of Mortain, the Conqueror's half-brother. One of his great Cornish manors was that of Alverton which, as Domesday Book itself recorded, had been held before the Norman Conquest by a certain Alward – hence its name of Alward's-ton (Alward's town.) It had probably been created as a manor by this Saxon lord, who was deprived of it by William I in favour of his half-brother. The entry in the Exeter Domesday relating to Alverton reads: 'The Count has I manor which is called Alwarton (Alverton in Madron) which Alward held T.R.E. (in the time of King Edward, who died January 5 1066). Therein are 3 hides of land, and they rendered geld for 2 hides. Sixty teams can plough these. Thereof the Count has in demesne (the home farm) half a hide and 3 ploughs and the villeins have 2½ hides and 12 ploughs. There the Count has 35 villeins and 2 borderers and 11 serfs and 1 rouncey and 17 unbroken mares (*equas indomitas*) and 9 beasts and 4 swine and 100 sheep and 3 acres of meadow and of pasture 2 leagues in length and in breadth. And it renders 20 *li* yearly and when the Count received it it was worth 8 *li*.' By comparison with other manors, Alverton was relatively populous and wealthy, being the only one in Cornwall which had increased in value – from £8 to £20 – with the Conquest. The phrase '11 serfs' probably signified 11 families or villages of serfs who, in reality, were slaves. Descendants of the 35 villeins became, during the next two centuries, freehold tenants who paid dues to the manor, a custom which has continued in a few places to the present day in small nominal payments by tenants to the lord of the manor. The hide was the unit of assessment on which the (Dane) geld was paid. It was equal to 192 Cornish acres (carucates) each of which contained 64 modern acres. In the case of Alverton, the hide and the plough appear to have been of equal extent. The manor house of Alverne was probably situated in Norman times in the valley between Lariggan River and Alverton at the western end of Penzance.

According to Charles Henderson the manor included in 1668 all Penzance, and Madron parish south of the church, inclusive of Heamoor, Tregavasson and Trewidden, the whole of Paul parish, all the south parts of St Levan, all St Buryan, Treeve and Sennen, Treveddra, Tregeseal, Bojewyan and Kegwin, all St Just, and about two-thirds of Sancreed parish.

After Robert Earl of Mortain, the manor of Alverton was held successively by Pomeroy, Richard Earl of Cornwall, and then by Terric Le Tyes, otherwise Tuetonicus, one of Richard's knights, member of a German family whose first representative in England was one of King John's military engineers. The Barons Le Tyes reputedly owned a small castle at Alverton, but their principal residence was Sherborne Castle, near Oxford. They made considerable efforts to develop the two small settlements of Penzance and Mousehole which by that time had sprung up within their Cornish estate, and succeeded in obtaining for both of them a number of charters. Penzance was then but an insignificant village, but Mousehole ranked as one of the largest ports in the county. In 1300 Henry, the first Baron Le Tyes, obtained from Edward I a charter for a weekly market on Tuesday at his manor of Mousehole. He died in 1308, and his successor, the third Henry and second Baron, was beheaded on 3 April 1321 for complicity in a rebellion against Edward II. His estates, after being forfeited to the Crown, were restored to Alice, his sister, who married Warine De L'Isle. In 1332 Alice, as lady of the manor of Alverton, successfully petitioned Edward III for a weekly market on Wednesdays and a seven days' fair at the feast of St Peter. 'Let all Penzance do honour to her memory', wrote Millett in 1876, 'for she was our lady patroness, and used her influence successfully in behalf of the town, at an early period of its history'.

Penzance owes a great deal to Alice De L'Isle, since this charter laid the basis of its future prosperity. The town also progressed in spiritual matters while under the benevolent sway of the Le Tyes family. When Cornwall was divided into parishes during the 11th century, Penzance had been included within the parish of Madron, the parish church being at the latter village nearly two miles distant. As Penzance grew the inconvenience and indeed injustice of this arrangement – a not uncommon grievance in Cornwall in mediaeval times – became increasingly felt, and to remedy it a chapel of ease was opened at Penzance. Some obscurity surrounds its date and location. By tradition, it was the chapel of St Anthony, at the western end of Barbican Street leading from the Quay to the Battery. After serving the religious needs of many generations of fishermen this small building was appropriately converted into a fish cellar. When the cellar was rebuilt around 1850 a badly mutilated cross from the old chapel was salvaged and placed in St Mary's churchyard, where it may still be seen. No records whatever exist of St Anthony's Chapel, but in 1429 a chapel of St Gabriel and St Raphael was licensed for Divine Service in Penzance; the presumption must be that this was a re-dedication of the old chapel of St Anthony.

In 1322 there existed in the manor of Alverton a chapel where Mass was daily celebrated by the Prior of St Michael's Mount and by the Rector of Madron, if the lord of the manor was present. Whether this was a private domestic chapel for the Le Tyes family or the chapel of St Mary, which stood on higher ground behind St Anthony's chapel, on the site of the present St Mary's church, is not clear. St Mary's chapel must in any case have already been in existence when licensed by Bishop Brantyngham in 1379; for at an enquiry during the reign of Henry VI (February 9, 1548-9) it was stated that Sir Henry Le Tyes, Knight, lord of the manor of Alverton – executed in 1321 – had founded a chantry in the Chapel of Our Lady, and endowed it with £4 out of the lands of the manor, for the salary of a priest to celebrate there. St Mary's was doubtless built as a replacement for St Anthony's, which no longer sufficed for the needs of the growing community.

Another chapel – that of St Clare, after which St Clare Street is named – lay in a field adjoining the present cemetery. A rental of Alverton of 1668 referred to 'a parcell of land adjoyning a certaine Chappell in the highway betweene Pensance and Madron Church – in the lord's hand'. Its date of foundation is unknown; a 'St Cleere's Lane' was mentioned in 1560 and again in 1600 – 'Synt Clears'. In 1845 Courtney stated that part of the chapel's foundations had recently been uncovered by the plough, and more of them afterwards laid open to show the shape of the building. Canon Doble identified the dedicatory saint as probably the popular Norman St Clarus of St-Clair-sur-Epte; the chapel doubtless owed this attribution to the Knights Hospitallers, to whom belonged both Newlyn and the parish of St Cleer, near Liskeard.

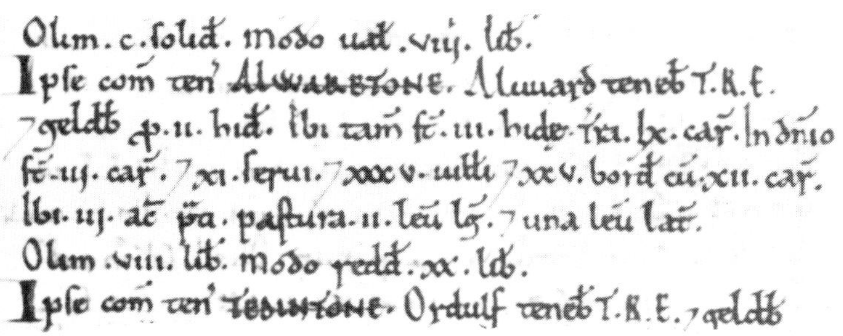
Olim. c. solid. modo uat. viij. lib.
Ipse com ten ALWARETONE. Aluuard tenebat T.R.E.
7 geldb p. ii. hid. Ibi tam st. iii. hide. Tra. lx. car. In dnio
st. iij. car. 7 xi. servi. 7 xxxv. uilli 7 xxv. bord cu. xii. car.
Ibi. iij. ac pa. pastura. ii. leu lg. 7 una leu lat.
Olim. viii. lib. modo redd. xx. lib.
Ipse com ten TEBIHTONE. Ordulf tenebat T.R.E. 7 geldb

Domesday Book entry relating to manor of Alverton. (PRO)

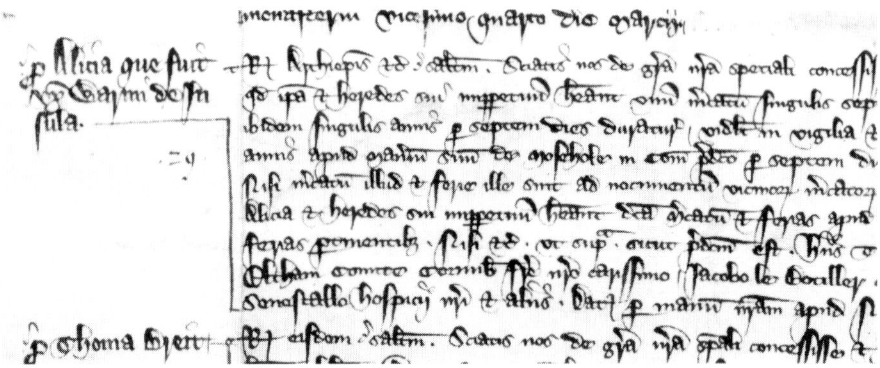

ABOVE and OPPOSITE ABOVE: Early 14th century charter relating to Penzance. (PRO) BELOW: Submarine Forest, Mount's Bay. (RIC/G)

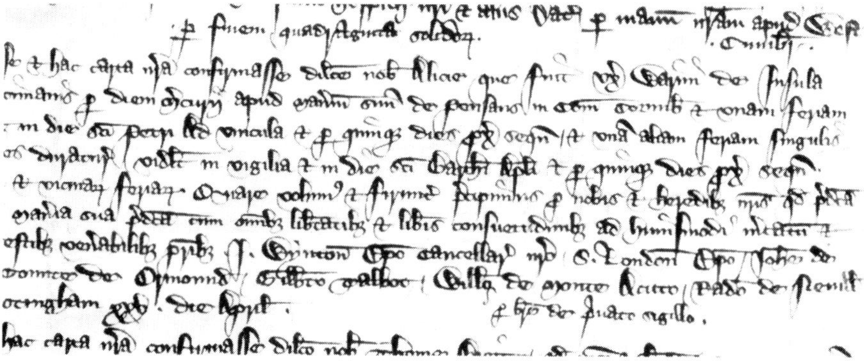

BELOW LEFT: Mutilated cross from the old Barbican chapel, now in St Mary's churchyard. (WT) RIGHT: When the Market cross was removed from Causewayhead in 1899, the inscription on its base, previously hidden from view, was again revealed.

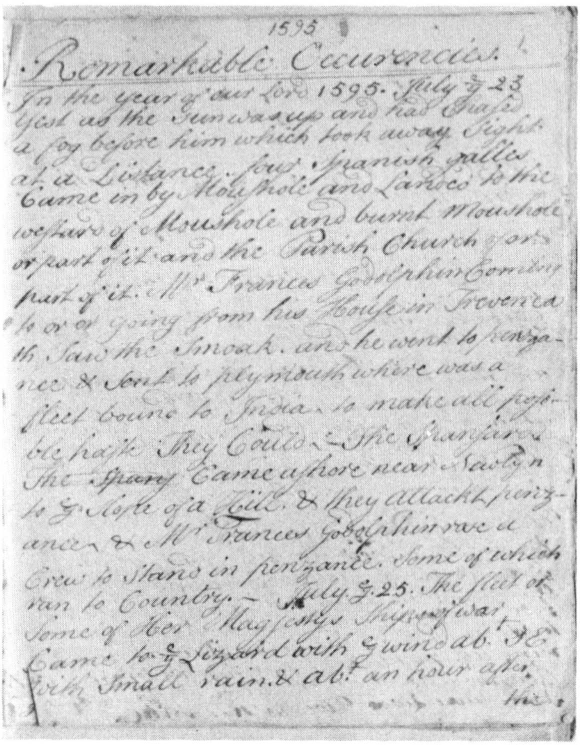

1595
Remarkable Occurrencies.
In the year of our Lord 1595. July ye 23
Just as the Sun was up and had Chased
a fog before him which took away Sight
at a Distance, four Spanish gallies
Came in by Mousehole and Landed to the
westward of Mousehole and burnt Mousehole
or part of it and the Parish Church or
part of it. Mr Francis Godolphin Coming
to or or going from his House in Trevenea
th Saw the Smoak. and he went to Penzance & sent to Plymouth where was a
fleet bound to India to make all possible hast They Could — The Spaniards
The Spany Came ashore near Newlyn
to ye Side of a Hill. & they attackt Penzance & Mr Francis Godolphin rac a
Crew to Stand in Penzance. Some of which
ran to Country. — July ye 25. The fleet of
Some of Her Magestys Ships of war
Came to ye Lizard with ye wind ab.t NE
with Small rain & ab.t an hour after
the

An account of the Spanish raid of 1595, written by William Williams, an old Newlyn fisherman in *Remarkable Occurrences or Principal Events.* (PMGL/WT).

The Growing Town

During the 15th century the population and trade of Penzance both increased following the peace with France. The town's fleet of merchant vessels grew in size and importance, and some particulars of these ships are recoverable from the records of Royal licences to their masters to transport pilgrims to the shrine of St James of Galicia (*ie* to Compostella). On landing in Spain the pilgrims had an overland journey of 35 miles with an armed escort of knights of the military order of St Jago to protect them from the Moslems. Shipboard conditions were equally grim, the travellers having to take their meals and sleep upon the ballast in the holds. Accordingly, the Pope decreed that the pilgrimage to Compostella should be equal to a voyage to Jerusalem. Charles V of France, to please subjects jealous of St James, procured for the abbey of Mont St Michel in Normandy, permission to grant indulgences to pilgrims.

The following vessels, all 'of Penzance' except when otherwise stated, were licensed for this pilgrimage, the number of pilgrims carried given in brackets: 1413, *Mary,* J. Russel of Fowey, master (50); 1434, *Michael,* 'of St. Michael's Mount', J. Williamson, master (40); 1434, *Michael* – presumably another vessel of the same name – J. Nicholl, master (80); 1440, barque *Katherine,* John Nicholl, master; 1445, *Michael,* Daniel Cosyn, master (60); 1445, *Margaret,* 'of Mount's Bay', Thos Vathy, master (40).

The traffic with Spain was by no means all one way. On 1 April 1458, an indenture between John Gybbes, of Penzance, and John Goffe, Spaniard, stated: 'John Goffe put himself to John Gybbes to be taught the art of fishing, to dwell with him as apprentice for 8 years, during which he shall serve him and Agnes his wife, who shall train and chastize him, according to the mode of the time, and shall give him 20s to the end. Witness Richard Boscawen, Robert Martyn and Robert Gascoyn'.

Many Bretons also lived in the district. At Madron, in 1431, there were 20 householders 'not born Englishmen', while 7 Bretons lived as servants in Penzance. In 1522 the Subsidy recorded 20 free landlords in Madron and 47 in Penzance, while 58 'paid on goods' – freemen. In Madron there were four Breton labourers, in Penzance 39 and four other Bretons. These figures provide a remarkable contrast with those of Domesday, when there were only a handful of freemen in the whole of Penwith. The richest man in Penzance and Madron was the vicar, who had £30 a year, and £100 of his own goods.

Meanwhile, the manor of Alverton continued in the hands of descendants of the Le Tyes family. Alice De L'Isle had a son, Gerard (1305-60); his son Warine (1333-81) was succeeded by an only daughter and heiress, Margaret, who carried the manor of Alverton to her husband Thomas, tenth Earl of Berkeley. In 1404 this Thomas Berkeley successfully petitioned the Crown for three fairs of two days each, thereby considerably augmenting the privileges previously granted to his wife's ancestress.

A charter of even greater import granted by Henry VIII in 1512 assigned all harbour dues to the town.

In 1537, despite the fact that England was not then at war with France, some French and Flemish cruisers had been committing serious depredations on our shipping, and Sir Thomas Seymour (the Queen's brother), Sir George Carew, Sir John Dudley and Christopher Coo (described as 'a rough English sailor') took command of a small fleet which had been quietly fitted out at Portsmouth. Froude's *History of England* tells how the people of Penzance, one August afternoon, heard the booming of distant cannon. Carew and Seymour, searching the western coast, had come up with four French warships on a plundering expedition. Closing with the marauders in Mount's Bay, they engaged them till nightfall, though heavily outnumbered. At daybreak one of the four was a sinking wreck, the others having slunk away under cover of darkness.

John Leland, Henry VIII's topographer, visited Mount's Bay around the year 1540. His snapshot glimpses of the locality are tantalisingly brief yet sharply revealing: 'Mousehole in Cornish is Portenis (Portus Insulae). [It] ys a praty Fyschar Town yn the West Part of Montesbay, lying hard by the Shoore, and hath no Savegard for Shyppes but a forced Pere. Also yn the Bay be Est the same Towne ys a good Roode for Shyppes cawled Guaves Lake . . . Pensants, about a Myle [2 miles] fro Mowsehole, stonding fast in the Shore of Montbay, ys the Westest Market Towne of al Cornwayle, and no Socur for Botes or Shyppes but a forsed Pere or Key . . . Marhasdeythyou [Market Jew, or Marazion] a great long Town burnid 3. and 4. anno Henr. 8. a Gallis [burned in 1512 by the French]. . . . The Paroch Chirch of Markine [St Hilary church] a Mile of. . . . In the North North-west [of St Michael's Mount] is a Peere for Bootes and Shyppes. . . . There hath bene much Land devourid of the Sea betwixt Pensandes and Mousehole. . . .'

In 1547, following the Reformation, the Royal Commissioners appointed by Edward VI to carry out the confiscation of chantries, themselves made a plea for the retention of St Mary's chapel at

Penzance, since it was 'dystaunte from the parishe church ij myles and halff . . . Mynystracion may not conveniently be spared, for if the people went daily to their parish church the towne would be in peril of burning by the Frenchmen and other enemies in tyme of warre'. The appeal went unheeded, and St Mary's was deprived of its endowment of 200 years before; but the Commissioners' warning proved prophetic, for the town was indeed burnt, not by the French, but the Spaniards.

Meanwhile the lives of Penzance people ran their personal and private courses. Little has come down to us, but just occasionally the veil is lifted. For example: at the Consistory Court proceedings in 1558 in relation to the breach of promise action between Cuthbert Marshall and Julianna Rougham of Penzance, widow, 'Nicholas Tredrey was present at Julianna's parlour at Pensans when she was betrothed to Cuthbert'. He went into the Hall where 'one Spannyerd and Nicholas Rawlen did sytt drykynge a quart of wyne which was set out of the doors – he desyred to borrowe their new goblet of wyne' and brought it to Cuthbert and Julianna, who pledged each other as husband and wife.

By 1550 the manor of Alverton had passed into the hands of Henry, Earl of Rutland but, following the Earl's death in 1553, it reverted to the Crown. On 8 January 1574 Queen Elizabeth granted a 21-year-lease in reversion of the tithes of Madron, Penzance and St Clare from Midsummer 1585 to Peter Coryton and William Hogben, together with parcels of land formerly belonging to the dissolved Priory of St John of Jerusalem. These Knights Hospitallers had owned an establishment at Landithy, in Madron. On 2 December 1584 the Queen leased to Thomas Betts, Gent, from Michaelmas 1584 a piece of land adjoining the cattle pound 'within our manor of Alwarton and Pensaunce', for sixpence per annum, with another waste parcel of land adjoining a chapel (St Clare) within the high road between Penzance and Madron, for fourpence per annum; and the Hemp Garden at the same place adjoining the house of John Beachym, Gent, lately in the occupation of Thomas Clies, at sixpence per annum. The manor was later granted to the Whitmore family, one of whom, Sir George Whitmore, sold it to Richard Daniel of Truro, whose daughter Mary became his wife.

Two great misfortunes befell Penzance during the later years of the 16th century. In the summer of 1578 the district was visited by the plague, the Madron burial registers sometimes recording as many as five burials a day during July and August.

While the effects of this were still fresh in people's minds they suffered another disastrous visitation – this time by Spanish raiders, who burned the towns of Mousehole, Newlyn and Penzance and spread terror around Mount's Bay. Richard Carew of Antony, in his great *Survey of Cornwall* (1602) began his description of the event with these memorable words: 'The three & twentieth of July, 1595. soone after the Sun was risen, and had chased a fogge, which before kept the sea out of sight, 4. Gallies of the enemy presented themselves vpon the coast, ouer-against Mousehole, and there in a faire Bay, landed about two hundred men, pikes and shot . . .'. The raiders burned the parish church at Paul, some houses round about, and the village of Mousehole whose inhabitants, fleeing before them, met Sir Francis Godolphin (of Treveneague, in St Hilary) on a green to the west of Penzance. He at once sent for assistance from captains in the vicinity and from Sir Francis Drake and Sir John Hawkins at Plymouth. Sir Francis Godolphin advised the people to retire to Penzance and prepare its defences while awaiting reinforcements; but though few in numbers and poorly armed they elected to march against the enemy.

By then the Spaniards had returned to their galleys and made a second landing at Newlyn, where they sent 400 pikes and shot up the hill to see what forces were ranged against them. Finding but a few men that had remained with Sir Francis, they marched on Penzance, their galleys firing on the retreating defenders. Sir Francis tried to rally his forces in the Market Place but, save for two resolute shot and about a dozen of his own servants, they all fled, forcing him to abandon the position; the Spaniards fired both Penzance and Newlyn. Towards evening, the Cornish forces, now 'encreased in nomber, and amended in heart', regrouped on Marazion Green. The enemy attempted to land again the following day, but met with so resolute a resistance that they gave up, while their galleys were forced away by bullets and arrows.

On 25 July Sir Nicholas Clifford, Sir H. Power, and other captains arrived with help from Plymouth; and some of Her Majesty's ships having reached the Lizard from Plymouth, the Spanish galleys took advantage of a change of wind from SE to NE to make a hasty departure. 'Thus haue you a summary report of the Spaniards glorious enterprise, and the *Cornish* mens infamous cowardise', concluded Carew somewhat censoriously, though he went on to excuse his countrymen by finding reasons for their failure – the unexpectedness of the attack, the advantage of the galleys' ordinance, and the absence of the men at sea or in the mines. Nevertheless, it is clear from other sources that the defenders largely owed their misfortune to their own lack of courage. Hatred for the Spaniards was long after felt in the district, and it used to be said that 'if you wish to try the temper of a Newlyn man, call him a Spaniard – and take the consequences'. But some of the inhabitants may have consoled themselves with the reflection that nothing could have averted the disaster, since it had been foretold in an old prophecy:

Ewra Teyre a war meane Merlin
Ara Lesky Pawle Pensanz ha Newlyn.

'There shall land upon the rock of Merlin
Those that shall burn Paul's Church, Penzance and Newlyn.'

ABOVE: Madron parish church, the mother church of Penzance. (WR/WT) BELOW: Mount's Bay from Gulval Carn. Drawn and engraved by William Willis, Penzance.

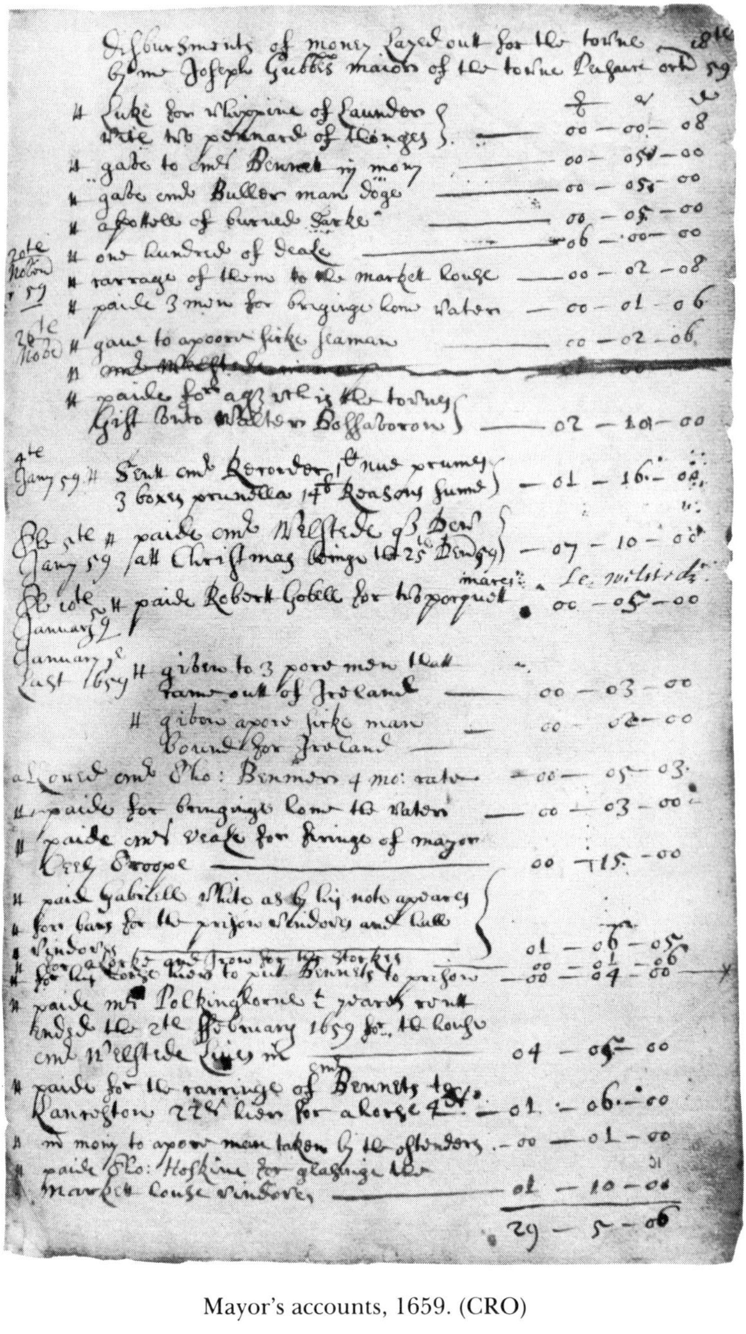
Disburstments of money layed out for the towne by me Joseph Gubbs maior of the towne Begune octo 59

Luke for whippinge of Launder with his pennard of thinges — 00 – 00 – 08
gave to mr Bennett in mony — 00 – 05 – 00
gave mr Buller man doge — 00 – 05 – 00
a bottle of burned sacke — 00 – 05 – 00
one hundred of deale — 06 – 00 – 00
carrage of them to the market house — 00 – 02 – 08
paide 3 men for bringinge home water — 00 – 01 – 06
gave to a poore sicke seaman — 00 – 02 – 06

paide for [illegible] given unto Walter [illegible] — 02 – 10 – 00
Sent mr Recorder [illegible] prunes 3 boxes [illegible] — 01 – 16 – 00
paide mr Westlede [illegible] at Christmas [illegible] — 07 – 10 – 00
paide Robert Gobell for his [illegible] — 00 – 05 – 00
given to 3 poore men that came out of Ireland — 00 – 03 – 00
given a poore sicke man bound for Ireland — 00 – 02 – 00
allowed mr Tho: Benmor 4 mo: rate — 00 – 05 – 03
paide for bringinge home the water — 00 – 03 – 00
paide mr Deake for [illegible] of mayor [illegible] — 00 – 15 – 00
paide Gabriell White as by his note appears for bars for the prison windows and hall windows — 01 – 06 – 05
for a locke and irons for the stockes — 00 – 01 – 06
for his horse hier to [illegible] Bennetts to prison — 00 – 04 – 00
paide mr Polkinghorne ½ yeares rent ended the 2th February 1659 for the house mr Westlede lives in — 04 – 05 – 00
paide for the carringe of mr Bennetts to Lanceston 22s hier for a horse 4d — 01 – 06 – 00
in mony to a poore man taken by the ostenders — 00 – 01 – 00
paide Tho: Hoskine for glasinge the market house windowes — 01 – 10 – 00
29 – 5 – 06

Mayor's accounts, 1659. (CRO)

Chartered for Success

There have been many examples in modern times of great cities totally devastated by war which, by the energy and determination of their inhabitants, have within a few years risen Phoenix-like from their ashes, prouder and more prosperous than before. In similar fashion the men of Penzance resolutely set to work after the Spanish raid to rebuilt their ruined town; and so successful were they that less than twenty years afterwards James I incorporated the Borough by charter on 9 May 1614. The Latin text sets out the townspeoples' reasons for desiring Borough status: 'our vill of Penzance is an ancient vill and port, both populous and of great force and strength to resist the enemies that shall there invade, and to defend the country there adjoining ... and is also a vill that exercised merchandise from time wherein the memory of man existeth not, and also having much commerce in and upon the high sea by means of the port of the same vill . . . And whereas the inhabitants . . . in times past have been manifestly burthened, and are daily heavily burthened with expense in fortification and defence of the vill aforesaid and of the port of the same, and in the maintenance, repair and support of divers sea fosses, banks, ways, and of a certaine piere or key formerly built . . . and all other necessary charges . . . especially in the taking and apprehending of pirates and marine felons and robbers upon the high sea . . . and very lately in the new erection and re-edifying the vill aforesaid, which was by the invasion of the Spaniards invidiously and in a hostile manner demolished and burnt to the injury of the inhabitants'.

The Corporation established by this charter consisted of a mayor, eight aldermen, and twelve 'assistants' (councillors.) John Madern was the first Mayor, Thomas Seyntawbin the Recorder and Thomas Rosewarne the Town Clerk. The names of the eight aldermen were John Clyes, John Game, Robert Dunkyn, Roger Polkinghorne, Joseph Lympanye, William Yonge, William Madern, jun, and Robert Luke. The twelve assistants were William Luer, Richard Sampson, Morice Roche, William Tompkyn, John Davye, Richard Bennett, Richard Fynney, David Penlease, Nicholas Game, Richard Trott, Richard Penquite, and Simon Hooper. In Madron church there is a slate memorial to John Maddern, son of the first mayor of Penzance, and a splendid brass to John Clies, elected its second Mayor in 1615, erected at the expense of his wife Blanche who, in a touching verse, declared that though 'God hath his soule, her heart his love still keepes'. Alas for human constancy – Blanche, who is portrayed with her husband on the brass, married again within a short time of her husband's death.

King James confirmed to Penzance the grant of harbour dues made by Henry VIII in 1512, and added to them the profits of the markets and fairs for an annual payment of five marks. The old Wednesday market was replaced by others on Tuesday and Thursday, while seven fairs were granted, including three new ones on the eve and day of Corpus Christi; the Thursday before St Andrew's Day, and the eve, day and morrow of St Bartholemew (apparently a revival and transference of the old Mousehole fair). Borough Justices were appointed, and a Court of 'Piepowder' (dusty feet) was established for the adjudgement of cases arising from the markets and fairs. The right was also given to hold land and property; and the new Corporation took advantage of it the following year to purchase from the lord of the manor of Alverton, Richard Daniell, 'one three corner plott of waste land, lyinge in the . . . town and village of Pensance . . . bounded on every part thereof with the King's hiye waye, and also all fayres and markets, and tolle stallage, package, coverage, etc., together with the stone peere or key' for £34 and a rent of 24s a year. The plot was a sloping piece of ground where, tradition says, the market was held before it came into possession of the the Corporation. Its exact extent is not known, but according to Courtney there was formerly a waste piece of ground between the higher and lower sides of Market Jew Street, which extended nearly as far as the old Alms House, where it came to a point. Till about 1800 there was a green bank almost on a level with the present terrace, where several trees grew on what is now the middle of the street. Being on the brow of the hill, it commanded a view of the whole bay before the surrounding area was built up; it was from this vantage point that Sir Francis Godolphin watched the progress of the Spanish raid. Here the Corporation built the attractive old Market House, demolished in 1836, but whose picturesque charm still lingers on in a well known engraving by Skinner Prout. Shops were soon after built on the three sides of the triangle, so giving the Market Place the shape it has to this day.

The 1614 charter defined the Borough Bounds as comprising all the ground lying within half-a-mile radius from the middle of the 'vill' or town. It was customary to make this measurement from the Market Cross standing (until 1829) in the old Market Place (which later became the Cattle Market and is now the Green Market); J. S. Courtney, in some notes reprinted in the *Cornish Telegraph* of 8 May 1867, put forward the view that this stone may not have marked the original spot whence the limits of half-a-mile round were determined, but from the centre of the present Market Place; 'this being more to the eastward, will explain the present inequality in the distances of the bound stone'.

Despite the enhanced civic and judicial powers granted by the charter, the district around Penzance remained turbulent and lawless. Among the State Papers is a letter of 7 February 1634-5, in which Sir James Bagg informed the Lords of the Admiralty that the endeavours of Mr Basset and other gentlemen in West Cornwall to save the cargo of the wrecked Spanish galleon which broke from her moorings in Gwavas Lake had been opposed by a riotous multitude consisting of the inhabitants of Mousehole and 'Marka-Jew' (Marazion), who maintained their unlawful proceedings with the cry of 'One and All!' threatening with death the servants of the Crown, and compelling them to avoid their fury by leaping down a high cliff.

In another letter of the same date from Ralph Bird, of Saltram, to Francis Basset, the rebels of Mousehole, with their fellow rebels of Market Jew, are said to have menaced the life of any officer who should come to their houses to search for certain hides that mysteriously disappeared from the deck of the galleon one boisterous night, and were probably transferred to Mousehole in the cock-boat of Mr Keigwin of that place; and various methods were suggested for administering punishment to the outrageous barbarians. In consequence of these complaints, the Lords of the Admiralty wrote to Sir Henry Marten on 12 February of the same year concerning the 'insolency' committed by the inhabitants of Mousehole and 'Markaiew', requesting that the offenders might be punished, and, if necessary, the most notorious of them sent to London for trial.

The granting of the King James charter, with its increase of powers and privileges for Penzance, acted as a further stimulus to the enterprise and industry of its people, and the town now began to forge steadily ahead, soon eclipsing its old competitor, Marazion. As early as 1250 Richard, King John's younger son, had confirmed to the Prior of St Michael's Mount three fairs and three markets at Marazion granted by previous kings. During the reign of Henry II Marazion sent two members to Parliament, a privilege Penzance was never to enjoy, and in 1595 it was given a charter of incorporation by Queen Elizabeth. The inhabitants of Market Jew must then have considered they had every chance of becoming the premier town in Mount's Bay, but if so they had reckoned without the initiative of their western neighbours. Marazion was soon complaining bitterly about the adverse effect of an alleged 'illegal' market set up at Penzance in opposition to its own; and it soon became obvious that the geographical position of Penzance, which made it the natural focus for trade from all West Cornwall, and the superiority of its harbour accommodation, would enable it to far outdistance its rival.

Before Penzance's dominating position was finally consolidated, however, its population had to undergo further severe trials. During the Civil War the town in common with most of of Cornwall – Saltash and St Ives were notable exceptions – declared for the King. Hals, in his *History of Cornwall,* described how in 1646 Penzance was punished for kindness to Lord Goring's and Lord Hopton's troop of horse, after they had been driven there by Sir Thomas Fairfax's Parliamentary forces. For two days the town was given over to plunder, and one of Fairfax's troopers – Edward Best of St Wenn – had as his share five gallons of English coin: silver and gold and pieces of eight. An oak door of an old building opposite the western end of the Market House survived into the 19th century complete with bullets fired by the Parliamentarians.

In 1647 the plague struck again in West Cornwall. The Madron registers show that its effects there (and at Penzance) were not quite as bad as at St Ives (500 dead). It flared up briefly again the following year at Madron and St Just.

In May 1648 Sir Hardress Waller defeated Royalist forces raised in Cornwall. An old manuscript by a Mr Mundy, of Penryn, describes the rising of the Penzance Royalists in June, to suppress whom forces under Col Bennett were sent 'who made short work, killed some, took some prisoners, scattered the rest (and) plundered the Towne . . . The victors passed through our's (*ie* Penryn) in a triumphant manner; viz. 1st – three souldiers, bearing upon the points of three swords, (carried upright) three silver balls used in hurling; then followed other three souldiers, marching very gravely in Aldermen's gownes; the souldiers marching after, with plundered ribbons and favours in their hats; ever and anon shooting off gunnes, seconded by a general shout and hallowing; then followed about forty prisoners; and after them, certaine horses laden with pillage, as feather-beds, household stuff, &c. In this manner they marched up St. Thomas-street, above the Fish Cross to the upper end of the Towne, on the lower side of the street, and down again on the upper end. The triumph being ended, the souldiers repaired to their quarters, and the prisoners to theirs, viz. – The Market-house'.

Alexander Daniell, of Lariggan (son of Richard Daniell of Truro, who had purchased the manor of Alverton from the Whitmores) in his *Briefe Chronologicall observaons of and for mine own ffamilie,* related how in 1648, 'ye Lord preserved my life at ye Penzance rout fro' a blody souldier that heav'd up his musket to knock me o' the head'. Alexander's son, Eliasaph, having been pressed into the Navy, served under Sir George Ayscough, admiral of the Commonwealth fleet which took the Scilly Isles from the Royalists in May and June 1651.

One of the most resolute Cromwellians in West Cornwall was Major Peter Ceely, of St Ives, who was vice-admiral and also commanded a troop of horse. He is reputed to have damaged, in an excess of puritanical zeal, much church property in the district, including Madron baptistry. His commission from Cromwell, 28 May 1655 to raise troops of horse is printed in Buller's now rare *Statistical Account of the parish of Saint Just in Penwith.* Orders were issued by him to Capt Francis Arundel a few years later when, following the death of Cromwell, the future looked uncertain for men of their persuasion:

'You are Imediatly to March wth yor Squadron to Penzance, and theire to quarter untyll ffather Order. In case any tumults or disturbbanse of the Peace of ye Nation, you are to suppress it the best way you may, and give mee an accompt from tyme to tyme as you have occasion, dated 4th. Jan., 1659.

P. Ceely.

'If you see occasion you may Quarter your squadron at St. Just, or ph. of St. (*sic*) or any other place that at Discretion keeping Intelligence with the Mount.

P. Ceely.'

This reference to the Mount is interesting. St Michael's Mount, after its sale by the Earl of Salisbury to Sir Francis Basset in 1640 was held first by him and after his death in 1645 by his brother Sir Arthur Basset, for the King. On 23 April 1646 Sir Arthur surrendered it without resistance to Parliamentary forces. Col John St Aubyn was appointed Captain of the Mount for Parliament the following year, and in 1659 purchased it from the by then impoverished Basset family; his descendants have lived there ever since.

The earliest year for which the Mayor's accounts have survived is 1655-6. They are headed: 'The towne of Penzance Debit to John Tremenheere Mayore of the towne for his disbursements in the tyme of his Mayoraltye ended the 3th October 1656'. The first item deals with the important question of water supply which was then conveyed into the town by open conduits: 'Payd ye 10th Octbr. 1655 to Luke Stephen to bring home the water . . .'. On 16 December a further sum was 'Pd. James Nuam (Newham) and 7 other men to Clense the leatt'. There are several entries relating to the cage, an instrument of correction in which malefactors were exposed to public view and ridicule, as in the stocks or pillory. On 29 December Thos Rawlings was paid 5s for 'meanding the cage', while on 24 April 1656 Nathaniell Trenery received 4s 9d 'for making iron worke about the cage and mending the Markett house locks'. The Borough Gaol also received attention: '13th ffebr. (1656) by 10 deale boards & timber for beames and nayles and worke mens wages for makeing a place in the lower prison for prisoners to lye, £2 4s. 6d'. One of the largest items of expenditure (£2 17s paid on 10 May) was to 'Mr. Edmond Hincks for the clocke larme [alarm or bell] & Diall', erected in the Market House, while on 22 May £1 13s 6d was paid to Ralph Searle 'to incompasse the larme and clocke' and for '2 pieces timber for the pentise [penthouse roof] with spukes and nayles and for his wages about it'. There are numerous other items relating to the Market House. On 10 January 7s was paid for 'a rope for the Markett', on 31 January 13s to 'Solomon the glasier for meanding the Markett house window'; on 15 May £4 10s 1d to 'Mr. Phi. Lanyon for Markett stuff'; on 20 May £1 13s 10d for '2 hhs. (hogsheads) of lyme, 9 C. of nayles, 200 of lafts & bringing sand & stones . . . to the Markett house', and £2 4s on 24 May to 'Jon. Samson & carne & there boy for 8 dayes worke in painting the Markett house'.

The Corporation's responsibilities for the harbour are reflected thus: '6th May. Made for the towne delivered the key wardens 3 halgh busshls and 2 pecks new & mending all the other measures, £1 12s 10d'. Inevitably, there are echoes of the still rather unsettled times which prevailed during John Tremenheere's mayoralty: '16th ffebr. to the constabells to put fourth the 6 men impressed and for the horses charge & mens charge & the constabells wth. them, £2 15s and 2th June. to Mathew Gover & others to goe to lands end & to the eastward, 1s 6d. . . . Ditto. spent one Captaine Arundle & the troops that morneing, 3s 6d'.

The Restoration of 1660 must have brought relief to the inhabitants of Penzance after the uncertainties of the Commonwealth. The Mayor's accounts for 1660-1 include: 'paide for makinke the Kinge's Armes in the towne hall, £3 2s 6d', and also reveal that the enormous sum of £14 10s was debited for Coronation expenses at Mr. Veale's on wine and beer. In May 1661 Catherine de Braganza, Charles II's Queen, arrived by sea at Gwavas Lake, thereby providing the town with another excuse for celebrations, and £1 15s was laid out on beer for the soldiers, £1 for the Queen's servants, and £4 7s 6d 'expended at the coming of the Queen'.

Taking advantage of its excellent record for loyalty during the Civil War, the town sought a valuable new privilege from the King by way of a coinage charter, the petition accompanied by a 'free present' to his Majesty. The charter was granted on 18 August 1663. The 'coinage' of tin was the practice of clipping a coin, or corner, from each block of metal for assaying purposes and the payment of dues, and stamping it with the Duchy seal. Penzance secured this privilege because most of the tin produced in the stannery of Penwith and Kerrier came from places far distant from Helston, the nearest coinage town, and the 'straightness [narrowness] and deepness of the wayes' by which it was conveyed greatly inconvenienced the tinners and added to their costs. Accordingly, 'Wee taking the said premises into our princely consideration, doe by these presents . . . nominate and appoint our towne of Pensance to be from henceforth for ever one of the Coynage townes within the said stannery'. A Coinage Hall was built on the eastern side of the Market House, which served until 1816, when the increased amounts of tin handled made necessary a larger hall near the Quay, where coining continued until its abolition in 1838.

In 1662 old St Mary's Chapel, which had suffered considerable damage during the Spanish raid, was rebuilt and enlarged. Three years later the Mayor and Corporation were granted a licence by Bishop Ward for divine service to be performed there, while in 1667 a bell was installed in the belfry at a total cost of £12 18s 6d. A plan of the building, dated 1674, shows that in the seating arrangements the sexes were separated, the women being in the centre and the men in the side aisles. The Mayor and Corporation, however, sat at the head of the women in the centre, the Mayor's seat occupying the place usually reserved for the altar, which in St Mary's stood beside the pulpit. In 1680 Mr John Tremenheere provided an endowment of £5 per annum from land at Leskinnick for the chapel, which was consecrated that same year. Some interesting correspondence passed between Bishop Thomas Lamplugh, of Exeter, and the Mayor (Thomas Benmer) and Corporation of Penzance. In a letter of 31 May 1680 the Bishop explained why the Church considered it desirable that buildings used for public worship should be dedicated by some solemn rites: 'So I do desire you to consider of this and prepare for the Consecration of your Chappell by setting some small pension upon it, that the Consecration may be performed about August next in my Visitacion: I will take care for a Sermon, and other things necessary for it; and doubt not but that you will so consider the honour of God, and the reputation of your Town, as to close with me in this . . '.

When informed of Mr Tremenheere's endowment he wrote again on 29 June, hoping that God would doubly and trebly repay it to him in blessings upon him and his. 'As for your beleef that the Chappell is already consecrated, you answer to the contrary in telling me that my Predecessors by licenses under their hands and seales have allowed Divine Services to be officiated there for so many yeares. For what needed such licenses if the place were as much consecrated as the mother church?' – *ie* Madron. In a third letter, written on 12 July, the Bishop said he hoped to be in Penzance on 28 August, and would perform the consecration the day after.

The Deed of Consecration stated that the church had been built by the townspeople's generosity, and that the Mayor and Corporation had given a piece of land for a burial ground. All fees and dues were to be paid to the Vicar of Madron. 'And lastly, the people of Penzance shall go to Madron Church when there is no service at St. Mary's, and always on the four great Festivals, and shall receive their Easter Eucharist at Madron.' The Vicar of Madron at this time was Reginald Trenayle, instituted 22 October 1662, who for some unknown reason was buried in the cloister of Westminster Abbey on 1 August 1700. He seems to have had little interest in his parish and failed to help the people of Penzance to find a suitable curate for St Mary's, hence an item of expenditure in the Borough Accounts, 1682-3, of £1 5s for 'expences on strange ministers that preached in the chappell'. The first curate at St Mary's was Stephen Lobb, who served there from 1699 to 1729.

The 17th century old Borough Accounts show with what eagerness great national events were seized on as excuses to indulge in mainly alcoholic celebrations. Examples are the peace treaties signed with Holland in 1667 and again in 1674; the annual bonfire lit on 29 May to commemorate Charles II's Restoration; and 'rejoicing at Munmouth's being routed' in 1685.

In 1670 £13 13s 2d was expended on 'two new masses for the towne', – the two silver maces still used on ceremonial occasions. 'Repairing the way from the New Street to the Sea, cauncing [causeying, or laying with small stones] carrying stones, &c', cost £5 19s 6d in 1678-9. A most unusual item in 1683 was £10 for 'Charges of a Lawsuit, and an inditement at the Assizes for an assault on the Mayor, by Mr William Maddern, allowed at a public hall, to be paid on the towne expense'. In 1687 £1 19s 6d was paid for 'four bound stones and carriage'. Millett says that one of these stones was set up 'at the end of the first row of houses at Wherry-town [now demolished] on the left hand side of the road leading to Newlyn, where it is sunk into the ground, since it obstructed the thoroughfare'. Another, at the foot of Alverton Lane, was similarly buried in May 1865 when widening operations left it isolated in the middle of the road. It was of granite, and in raised letters on the western side was P (for Penzance), on the south 16 and on the east 87 (making the date 1687), while the north side, which had been against the hedge, was blank. When the stone was removed, a pit was dug into which a block of granite was lowered. In the block was deposited a hermetically sealed glass jar containing a scroll recording the circumstances of the boundstone's removal. The old stone was then laid on top and covered in. A new pillar, erected 13′ 6″ north of the old site, indicated where its predecessor had been buried. The ceremony was performed in the presence of the Mayor (Mr F. Boase) and the Chairman of the Madron Local Board, Rev M. N. Peters. Hopes were mutually expressed that any jealousy between Penzance and Madron might be as effectually buried as the old boundstone, and that reciprocal interests and friendship would firmly unite the mother parish and her borough daughter! Two other boundstones erected in 1687 still occupy their original sites; these are at Chapel St Clare, on the right of the road leading to Madron, and at Chyandour, on the left of the road leading to Gulval.

In 1687 James II called in many of the old borough charters on the pretext of checking their validity, his real object being to extort money. The Penzance charter of 1614 was taken to London for examination, and being proved valid was returned in a trunk. This little episode cost the Corporation £159 17s 4d in expenses of one kind and another. By such acts of oppression James II made himself extremely unpopular. One of James' most determined opponents, Bishop Trelawny, who with Archbishop Sancroft and six other bishops had been committed to the Tower in 1688, was entertained at Penzance on 12 August 1692; 'Treating the Bishop and Major General Trelawney at Newman's', £6 16s 4d. A popular refrain of the day,

And shall Trelawny die?
Here's twenty thousand Cornish bold will know the reason why,

was many years afterwards incorporated into a well known song by Rev R. S. Hawker, of Morwenstow, which has become the county's 'national' anthem.

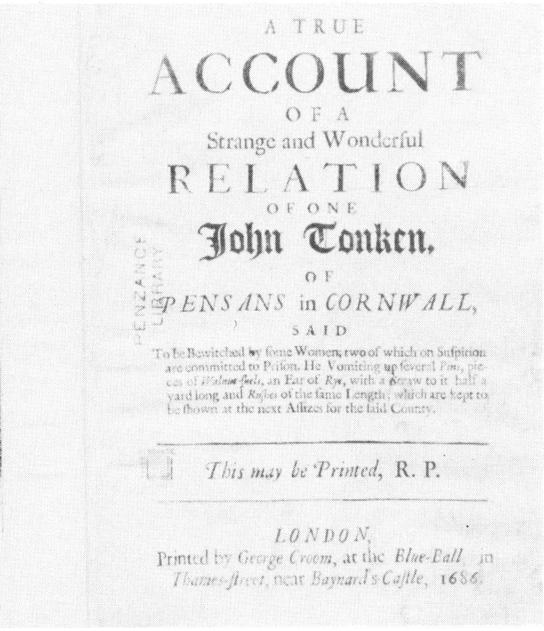
A TRUE
ACCOUNT
OF A
Strange and Wonderful
RELATION
OF ONE
John Tonken,
OF
PENSANS in CORNWALL,
SAID
To be Bewitched by some Women, two of which on Suspicion are committed to Prison. He Vomiting up several *Pins*, pieces of *Walnut-shels*, an Ear of *Rye*, with a Straw to it half a yard long and *Rushes* of the same Length; which are kept to be shown at the next Assizes for the said County.

This may be Printed, R. P.

LONDON,
Printed by *George Croom*, at the *Blue-Ball* in *Thames-street*, near *Baynard's Castle*, 1686.

Alleged witchcraft at Penzance. This narrative was attested by Peter Jenken, Mayor of Penzance in 1685, and John Geose, Justice. (PMGL)

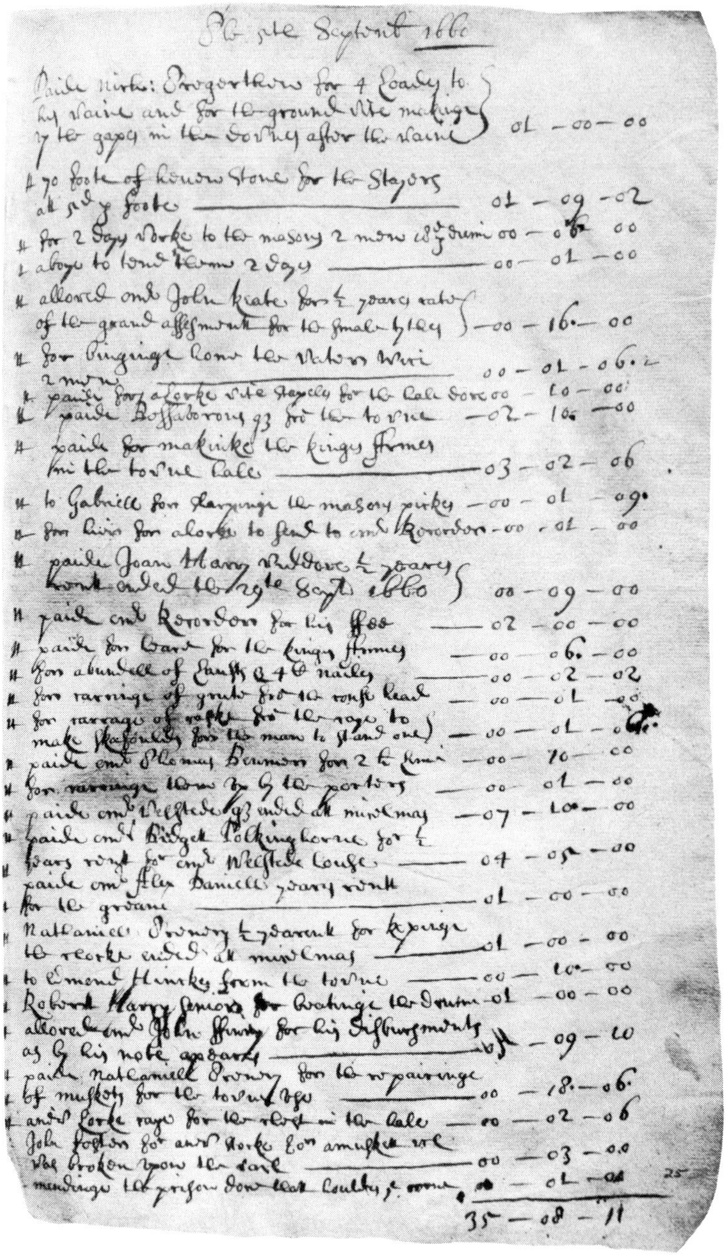

Sbr 29the Septembr 1660

Paide Nicho: [illegible] for 4 Loades to his waine and for the ground vse makinge vp the gapes in the downes after the waine — 01 – 00 – 00

for 70 foote of [illegible] stone for the Stayers att 5d y foote — 01 – 09 – 02

for 2 dayes worke to the masons 2 men 18d p diem — 00 – 06 – 00

a boye to tend them 2 dayes — 00 – 01 – 00

allowed mr John Keate for ½ yeares rate of the grand assessment for [illegible] — 00 – 16 – 00

for bringinge home the water [illegible] 2 men — 00 – 01 – 06

paide for a locke [illegible] for the hale dore — 00 – 10 – 00

paide [illegible] for the towne — 02 – 10 – 00

paide for makinge the kinges Armes in the towne hall — 03 – 02 – 06

to Gabriell for sharpinge the masons pickes — 00 – 01 – 09

for hire for a horse to send to mr Recorder — 00 – 01 – 00

paide Joan Harry widdowe ½ yeares rent ended the 29th Septr 1660 — 00 – 09 – 00

paide mr Recorder for his ffee — 02 – 00 – 00

paide for board for the kinges Armes — 00 – 06 – 00

for a bundell of Lathes & 4 c nailes — 00 – 02 – 02

for carringe of [illegible] for the [illegible] — 00 – 01 – [illegible]

for carriage of [illegible] for the [illegible] to make scaffoldes for the man to stand one — 00 – 01 – [illegible]

paide mr Thomas [illegible] for 2 [illegible] — 00 – 10 – 00

for carringe [illegible] by the porters — 00 – 01 – 00

paide mr Westlake [illegible] ended att michelmas — 07 – 10 – 00

paide mrs Bridget Polkinghorne for ½ years rent for mr Westlake house — 04 – 05 – 00

paide mr Alex Daniell yeares rent for the Greene — 01 – 00 – 00

Nathaniell Downey ½ yeares rent for keepinge the clocke ended att michelmas — 01 – 00 – 00

to Edmond Hinkes from the towne — 00 – 10 – 00

Robert Harry senior for beatinge the drum — 01 – 00 – 00

allowed mr John Harry for his disbursements as by his note appeares — [illegible] – 09 – 10

paide Nathaniell Downey for the repairinge of muskets for the towne use — 00 – 18 – 06

and [illegible] for the [illegible] in the hale — 00 – 02 – 06

John Foster for [illegible] a musket wch was broken upon the [illegible] — 00 – 03 – 00

mendinge the prison dore [illegible] — 00 – 01 – [illegible] 25

35 – 08 – 11

Mayor's Accounts, 1660. (CRO)

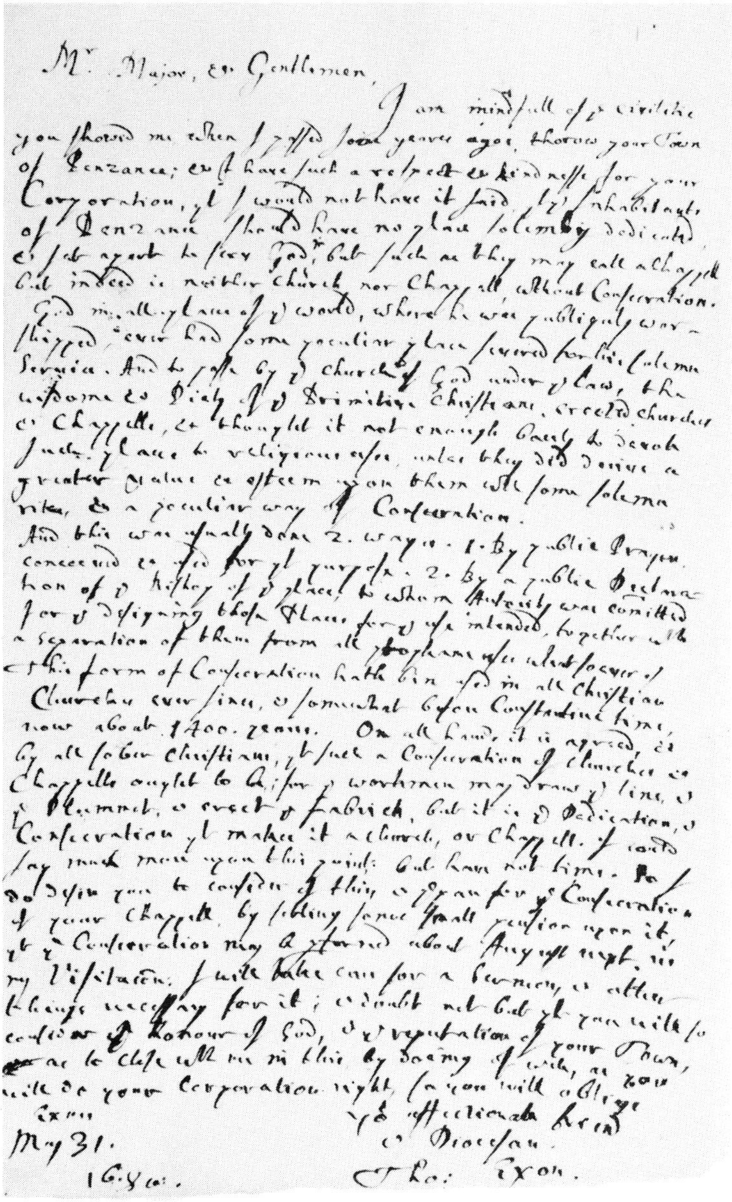

Mr. Major, & Gentlemen,

I am mindfull of ye civilitie you showed me when I passed some yeares agoe, through your Town of Penzance; & I have such a respect & kindnesse for your Corporation, yt I would not have it said, ye Inhabitants of Penzance should have no place solemnly dedicated & set apart to serve God in, but such as they may call a Chappell but indeed is neither Church nor Chappell, without Consecration. God in all places of ye world, where he was publiquely worshipped, ever had some peculiar place severed for his solemn Service. And to passe by ye Church of God under ye law, the whome ye Piety of ye Primitive Christians, erected Churches & Chappells, & thought it not enough barely to devote such places to religious use, unlesse they did derive a greater value & esteem upon them wth some solemn rites, & a peculiar way of Consecration. And this was usually done 2. wayes. 1. By publiq Prayers conceived & used for yt purpose. 2. By a publiq Declaration of ye Bishop of ye place, to whom Authority was comitted for ye designing those places for ye use intended, together wth a separation of them from all prophane uses whatsoever. This form of Consecration hath bin used in all Christian Churches ever since, & somewhat before Constantine's time, now about 1400. yeares. On all hands, it is agreed, & by all sober Christians, yt such a Consecration of Churches & Chappells ought to be; for ye workmen may draw ye line, & ye plummet, & erect ye fabrick, but it is ye Dedication, & Consecration yt makes it a Church, or Chappell. I could say much more upon this point: but have not time. I do desire you to consider of this, & prepare for ye Consecration of your Chappell, by settling some small pention upon it, yt ye Consecration may be performed about August next, in my Visitacon; I will take care for a Sermon, & other things necessary for it; & doubt not but yt you will so consider ye honour of God, & ye reputation of your Town, as to close with me in this, by doing of which, as you will do your Corporation right, so you will oblige

Exon

May 31.

1680.

Yr affectionate frend

& Diocesan

Tho: Exon.

Letter sent by the Bishop of Exeter to the Mayor, Thomas Benmer and Corporation of Penzance, 31 May 1680. (CRO, WT)

ABOVE: Mousehole, general view, (PL) and BELOW: harbour.

A Place of Considerable Note

In the early 18th century Penzance temporarily lost the charter it had so expensively retained during the reign of James II. In 1703 Mr John Carveth, an attorney, was elected Chief Magistrate of the Borough, but having once tasted the fruits of office he refused to surrender them on the expiry of his term, and 'stood in Mayor by force and violence for three years' in defiance of the rules. Inevitably, the Borough charter was forfeited. However, a majority of the aldermen and assistants successfully petitioned Queen Anne to restore their former rights, liberties and franchises. A majority of the aldermen and assistants were required to meet and elect a mayor from among their number, 'likewise commanding John Borlace and Francis Paynter, Esqrs., Christopher Harris, Francis Paynter, and John Penneck, Gentlemen, that they or two of them should be present at the said election' to act as commissioners.

The Corporation duly met and chose Alderman William Tonkin, a merchant, and one of Carveth's principal opponents. The Borough Accounts for the next few years contain several curious entries: 'Expences in seeking Mr. Carveth, £1 14s' and 'On serving Mr. Carveth with the Mandamus at Newman's, 5s.' 'On demanding the regalia from Mr Carveth, 4s 6d' and 'Charges on putting the pretended constables to Bodmin, £10'. These constables, sworn in by Carveth, had acted illegally during his usurpation, and were presumably sent to Bodmin to stand trial. The total expenses incurred by the Corporation imposed a severe strain on their revenues for some time after.

In 1710 a school was established by George Daniell, son of Alexander Daniell, at Madron, for the education of 60 poor boys and girls from Penzance, Madron and Morvah, the endowment being in lands near Penzance. The original schoolroom and master's house adjoin Madron churchyard. Soon afterwards (1711) a school was started in Penzance by J. Buller of Morval but, as the endowment was provided from a fixed term Government annuity, the school closed when this ceased to be paid.

The once celebrated Penzance Grammar School, whose pupils included Sir Humphry Davy and Davies Gilbert, may possibly have been set up to take its place. The earliest known reference to the Grammar School occurs in 1728, when it was already a well established institution. Its masters were usually curates at St Mary's.

In 1713 the Corporation spent £5 celebrating the Peace of Utrecht, proclaimed on 4 May. They also allowed £7 5s in 'expence at Mr. Pellow's' on proclaiming George I in 1714, and an even larger sum (£14 14s 7d) at his Coronation, while £1 5s in cash was given to 'the mob'. A large item in 1721-2 was £40 as 'the Mayor's allowance for Serjeants' cloaks, hats and other expences inseparable from the Mayoralty'; and two years later fourteen yards of 'blue shalloon' – a French woollen fabric of twill weave – were purchased as lining for the Mayoress's seat. An interesting item in the accounts of James Hawkey, Mayor in 1723-4, runs: 'To expences in sending a hue and Cry to St. Ives, 3s'. During the following year one entry seems to presage trends towards sex equality in the modern church: 'to a poor clergy-woman, 2s'.

Around 1725-30 some alterations were made at St Mary's, the chancel being extended across the eastern end of the building. 'To cash spent with Dr. Borlase [Dr Walter Borlase, Vicar of Madron], Messrs Tonkin and others, about enlarging the Chappell, £6', and 'Subscription for enlarging the chapel, £100'. In 1727 £12 was spent at 'Lewellin's' in celebrating the Coronation of George II and Queen Caroline, and on gunpowder, tar barrels and cyder. On 23 December the Corporation made an effort to have the town's postal service improved by getting a post three times a week, and a petition was later drawn up and and presented to Lord Falmouth, the Recorder. That gentleman resigned the recordership shortly afterwards, and was succeeded by his son, the 'expenses at Lewellings' amounting to £5 13s.

In 1729 the tinners rioted in several parts of the county, the cause, as usual, being the scarcity and dearness of corn. The Redruth tinners marched on St Ives, where an engagement took place in which several were killed. There were also disturbances at Redruth, St Michael's Mount and other places. Penzance, a port from which grain was shipped, and near the St Just mining district, put itself in a state of readiness in case of trouble. A 'guard' was obtained, with 'shot and bullets', while twelve firearms, bayonets and cartouch boxes, bought in London by Henry Hichens for 12 moidores (then worth £17 11s) were sold to the Corporation for only £8 2s in 1729 on 25 April. 'To Disbursments paid by the Constables abt. the Soldiers as pr. Rect., 10s 2d' and 'To Expence paid Roop for the Guards placd. at the end of Market jew Street as pr. Rect., £2 9s 6d.' 28 May, 'To the Constables Disbursmts. about the Souldiers in candles & horse hire & a Guide wn. (they) went of as pr. their Acct. & rect., 15s 1½d'. The soldiers were billetted in a room above the Coinage Hall, provided by William Harry, and supplied with straw at a cost of £1.

During the 1730s Penzance was much concerned by an attempt by Penryn to gain status as a coinage town, and gave two large sums, one of £9 12s 6d and the other of £21 12s 7d to Mr G. Borlase for successfully opposing it. In 1733-4 occurs this oddity: 'To Pasco Biscay, for carrying cendars under the Aldermen's and Assistants' seats, 2s 6d' which Courtney explains by referring to the foreign custom of placing pans of charcoal under seats in severe weather. A year later Mr H. Hichens was paid £1 7s for 'Mr Harold's passage', he being the new schoolmaster, while the school room was put in order at a cost of £34 6s.

One pleasant old custom regularly observed at Penzance was that of maypole dancing; in 1739 John Jenkin was paid a guinea for a spar for the maypole. A far less attractive practice is recalled by this entry of 8 February 'To Thomas Pidwell, for a woman's bridle, 10s 6d'. One wonders if this was to curb the scolding tongues of some of the local fisherwomen who, by all accounts, were sometimes rather free with their badinage and abuse. War with Spain was declared on 19 October 1739 and, with bitter memories of the town's unpreparedness in the 1595 raid, the decision was taken to erect a battery on the 'holy headland' of Pen Sans, where the War Memorial now stands. This proved an expensive undertaking: 1740-1 – 'Expenses about building the Battery, £214 1s 0d' and 'Expenses drawing the guns into the Battery, 5s 8d' with 'To Peter Downing, an Ensign-staff and colours for the battery, 5s'. Precautions of another kind were taken in 1743 with the purchase of a fire engine for £8 7s 6d and twelve leather buckets the following year for £2 3s. In 1744-5 a piece of ground for the chapel yard was purchased from Mr Richard Hichens for 5s, while a year later 'expenses at Hitchcock's when the southern part of the Chapel-yard was consecrated by my Lord Bishop of Exon' amounted to £8 2s 6d.

In the 1740s John Wesley and his brother Charles visited the Penzance area. They encountered a great deal of opposition from the Vicar of Madron, Rev Dr Walter Borlase of Castle Horneck, brother of Dr William Borlase, the historian and antiquary. As a zealous magistrate Walter Borlase was much exercised in seeking out Papists, Jacobites and others disaffected to the existing Church and State establishment. He regarded the Wesleys and their followers with the greatest hostility, and was relentless in his persecution of them. It has become rather fashionable to find excuses for the Doctor's brutal conduct towards these entirely harmless people; but one finds it difficult to condone such actions as his incarcerating Thomas Maxfield, a preacher, in the notorious Penzance gaol to await impressment into the navy, on the specious grounds that he was 'of no lawful calling or sufficient maintenance'. There was something of the tyrant in the make-up of this man who the puzzled John Wesley himself allowed was otherwise 'a person of unquestioned sense and learning'.

On 30 July 1744 Charles Wesley wrote in his *Journal:* 'I cried to a mixed multitude of wakened and unawakened sinners near Penzance, "Is it nothing to you, all ye that pass by?" I prayed with the still-increasing flock whose greatest persecutor is their Minister. He and the Clergy of these parts are much enraged at our people's being so ready in the Scriptures. One fairly told Jonathan Reeves [a lay itinerant] he wished the Bible were in Latin only, that none of the vulgar might be able to read it. Yet these are the men that rail at us as Papists!'.

On several occasions Wesley preached on the cliff at Chyandour. He wrote on 1 September 1774 that at Penzance, 'when the people here were as roaring lions, we had all the ground to ourselves; now they are become lambs'. Two years later he preached to a huge congregation from a gentleman's gallery which commanded the Market Place. His last visit to the town took place on 24 August 1789 when, being a rainy afternoon, he was obliged to speak in the new 'preaching house, considerably the largest and, in many respects, far the best, in Cornwall'.

In 1745 the country was thrown into a state of alarm by the Jacobite Rebellion. The Young Pretender was not without sympathisers in Cornwall, and George Borlase raised an Independent Company of Volunteers at Penzance, armed with muskets which had been seized by George's brother Walter from the *Charming Molly* privateer wrecked at St Michael's Mount. However, the rising failed, and the victory gained by British troops over the Jacobites under Charles Edward at Culloden on 16 April 1746 was celebrated at Penzance by drinking the Duke of Cumberland's health; while Admiral Anson's defeat of the French fleet off Cape Finisterre in the summer of 1747 was marked by a gift of £1 3s 6d 'to the independent company, and gunners.' A singular item entered on 17 November 1747 read: 'Paid for Wood to burn Moses Morgan's Cow, 1s 5d'. Presumably the animal was a victim of the cattle plague, or foot-and-mouth disease, as it is now called. Also 1s was paid for 'removing the Deads from the Old Cage'. It would seem to have become filled with rubbish, 'deads' being a mining term for waste rock. Finally, 'Paid for cutting some new springs, and bringing more water to the town, £3 15s 1d'.

Around 1750, 233 laces of ground were cut down to widen the road at Chyandour Cliff; £2 10s was given to T. Woodis and Son for measuring the ground, and to the labourers. When Bishop Lavington visited Penzance a few years later the streets were swept before his entrance at a cost of 2s, while S. Bennets' bill for entertaining him came to £19 17s 3d. An amusing item in 1753-4 was a payment of £1 to R. Scadden for cleaning, varnishing, gilding and 'altering the wrong spelling of the King's arms in the Town hall'. Among charitable payments made in 1756-7 were: 'To Curing

Branwell of two large Wounds in his Head & Contusions of his Neck and Shoulders, £2 2s.'

In October 1757 a cartel – that is, a captured British ship freed for carrying released prisoners for exchange – arrived at Penzance. 'To 37 Prisoners landed out of the Barrington Sloop a Cartel from Bayonne John Grant Commander 37s. Robt. Turner Do. ye 4th 2s. & to Francis Lanyon's Widow for Lodging one of them 1s. – £2.' 'To Denis Pendegras, Richd. Heath, Joseph Mead & Hugh Allen Sick Prisoners with Passes, 4s'. Other notable items that year were: 'To the Cryer for whipping a Vagrant Is. And for cleaning the Corn Market House, Is.'; 'To E. Sampson the Singer 1 Year's Salary, £1 1s'; 'To Rich. Stone for Coals for the Guard Room, 5s 10d'; and on 9 November ; 'To Mr. Rawles for Candles for Do., 4s 10d'; on 26 November; 'To Catherine Hore a Soldier's Wife big with Child to redeem her Clothes, 5s.' 'To Solomon Richards for putting her Part of the Way to Modbury to her Husband, 10s 6d;' 'To Michael Howard Carrying Gravel on the Foot Way upon the Cliff, 2s.' On 23 January 1758 'To a Soldier's Wife with 2 Children & a bad Breast to travel to Falmouth to her Husband, 5s;' and 'To Edwd. Gandy 2 Days Wheeling Stone out of Thos. Pidwell's Field into the High-way & making up Nichs. Cloak's Hedge, 2s 2d'.

On 22 October 1759 the town incurred charges of £1 11s 6d, 'on Acct. of two Defecter'. A curious item from 1760 reads: 'To 2 Men Watching ye Reservoir & Market Ho. at Shrove Tide, 2s 6d'. This was to prevent damage caused by unruly youngsters. On 23 April 1760. 'To 3 Men Watching the French Prisoners & Expences, 4s 6d'.

A most alarming event took place that year when an Algerine corsair called the *Cavallo Bianco* (White Horse) was wrecked near the Chimney Rock on the south side of Penzance, and the town found itself acting as unwilling host to the barbarous crew. Several descriptions of this remarkable incident have been preserved, but the most vivid was that written by an eye-witness to a friend and first published by D. Philp, of Falmouth, in No 25 of the *Cornish Magazine* for January 1828.

'On Sunday, the 28th of September, about two o'clock in the morning (when by the course of nature all things would have been wrapped in the most profound darkness, had not the silver beams of the Moon, then walking in brightness befriended us), I was awakened out of a sweet sleep, by the terrific sound of a drum beating "To Arms." . . . I was at first informed that a French man-of-war was driven on shore, and that upwards of fifty men, armed, were marching through the Town; but soon after I was told that an Algerine Xebecque was stranded just below the Town, and that the crew had the Plague on board; and a further account was, that they were swimming to land as fast as possible. Was not my consternation, think you, great? These shocking accounts were succeeded by the ringing of the Town Bell, the confused clamour and din of the men and the screaming and shrieks of the women (the greater part of whom had quitted their beds in dreadful dismay). The night continued very bright (the Moon having been full on the 25th). A general assemblage of the inhabitants now took place in the Market plot, to Consult on the best method of preventing the infected Turks from coming into the Town. After a long deliberation it was agreed that the Independent Company commanded by Captain George Borlase should arm themselves, and if it could be ascertained that the Plague had been on board, they should fire at and kill the unfortunate men before they could reach the Shore. This severe resolution however was not executed, as in the interval of Consultation, the greater part of the shipwrecked mussulmen had swam safely to the shore, and some had entered houses at the Quay. . . . Out of one hundred and seventy-two, fourteen were drowned. The dead bodies were subsequently thrown on shore and buried in the adjoining sands. Amongst the crew were five Christians, one Irish, one Spanish, and three Portuguese. As soon as possible after the unfortunate sufferers got on shore, they were accommodated . . . and they have been since treated with the greatest attention and humanity . . . In the Course of the day, notwithstanding it was Sunday, the vessel was cut to pieces by our savage neighbours, and very few things were saved by the distressed crew. Indeed as it was a Corsair or Piratical vessel, there were few articles of value on board, except scimitars and guns ornamented with silver. The Captain's name is Amida Benzgonda – a little man – with a fierce countenance – and an eye that seems to flash fire. He expressed great joy, as all the Turks and Moors did on their being informed that they were driven on shore on the Coast of England. Two expresses have been received by the Mayor from Mr Pitt, the one ordering that the Algerines should perform a strict quarantine, the other that all the clothes, guns and scimitars which can be found should be carefully kept for them. A letter has also been received from Admiral Boscawen, stating that the Hind sloop of war of twenty guns and a Transport will soon be sent down to convey the Turks from hence to Algiers. I had this day an opportunity of witnessing the embarkation of the Turks and Moors . . . Two large boats were sent from the Transport to take them from Cribenzawn Rocksı but though sixty soldiers attended to assist the seamen, it was not effected without great reluctance and resistance . . .!'

The transport took them from Penzance to Falmouth. As the Turks were confined under quarantine while at Penzance, they were unable to do much mischief but, being allowed their liberty at Falmouth, they frequently walked to Penryn and stole shirts from the hedges and indeed everything they could lay their hands on.

Some seamen belonging to a Portuguese vessel going alongside the transport were assailed by the Turks, and many of them dreadfully wounded. By government order, they were treated with more lenience than their behaviour merited, and were conveyed by *La Blonde*, a captured French frigate, in safety back to Algiers at considerable expense. Several entries relating to this incident occur in the Borough Accounts: 7 October 1760 – 'To the Man that came Express from Admiral Boscawen, £1 1s' and 'For the Post for stopping to write Mr Pitt about the Turks. Algerines, Is'.

Further improvements to the town's eastern approach were made in 1763. £17 12s was paid to John Rogers 'for his Land taken into the high way on the Cliff', while James Tonkin received 12s 6d for one year's rent and £18 15s for the purchase of 25 laces of land at the same place. George Cunnack was paid £9 for the lease of a house pulled down there, and Mary Cunnack and Ann Edmonds, widows, £4 4s for the lease of a killing shop; 'To Sampson Branwell for the purchase of the said Killing Shop and Pound behind it and Fifteen feet of Land more taken into the high way, £4 16s 6d'. Many and varied calls continued to be made on the Borough's charity, and genuine cases never seem to have been refused. 'To the Widow of one James Wearne who came here by a pass from Plymouth to Enquire after her husband's Settlement being very big with Child and greatly Distressed, 4s' and on 20 December 'To Thomas Williamson, Master of the Prince Henry of London and Eight Mariners Wrecked in the North Channel and Landed at Mousehole with a pass for London, 5s'.

In *A Description of England and Wales*, printed for Newbury and Carnan 'London' 1769, Penzance was described as 'a place of considerable note; many of the Cornish gentry have houses here, and a great trade is carried on by the inhabitants, who are owners of several ships. The town consists of about six hundred houses [and] the streets are paved . . .'. Penzance was indeed thriving. Fish, tin and copper were largely exported, and both the markets and fairs were in a flourishing condition. Society, however, still showed a certain lack of refinement during the early part of George III's reign. Cock fighting, smuggling and hard drinking were, despite the influence of the Wesleys, freely indulged. Travelling was usually by horse, and goods were transported by pack horses and mules. Carpets were unknown, except among the wealthy, sanded floors being the rule, and there was not a silver fork in the town. A Mrs Treweeke, through whose influence the Assembly Rooms at the rear of the Union Hotel were built, was the first person in Penzance who possessed a carpet. She also owned a carriage; so rare were these vehicles that when she rode out in it to attend a concert at St Ives, where some of the inhabitants knew as much about concerts as carriages, she was followed on her arrival by an admiring crowd, shouting 'The concert is come! the concert is come!'.

But manners, wealth and knowledge were improving all the time. A Ladies' Book Club was formed in 1770 and a Gentlemen's Book Club soon after, while the Grammar School was re-established by the Corporation in a new building in 1789. But perhaps the most convincing proof of the high cultural standing of Penzance in the closing years of the 18th century is the fact that two Presidents of the Royal Society – Davies Gilbert and Sir Humphrey Davy, the one an all-round scientist and historian, the other one of the greatest chemists this country or the world has ever produced – were nurtured during their early years in its stimulating atmosphere.

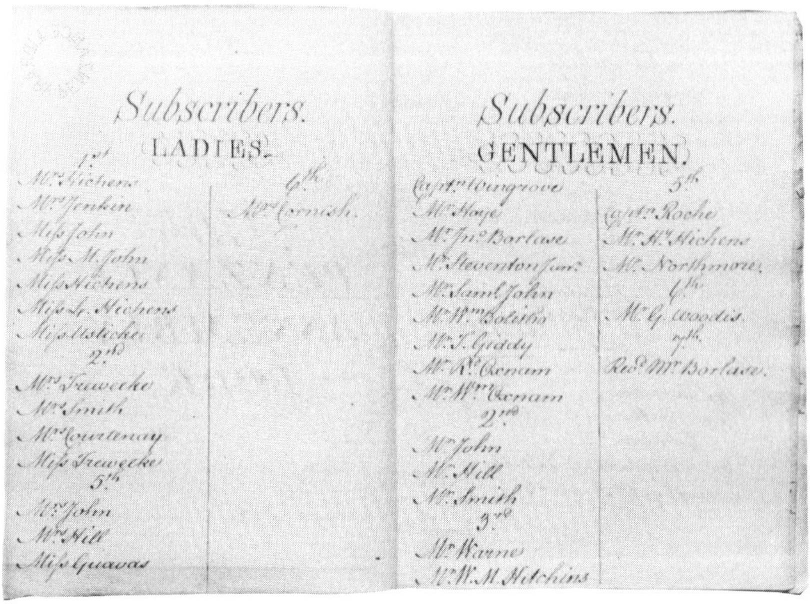
Subscribers.
LADIES.
1st
Mrs Hichens
Mrs Jenkin
Miss John
Miss M. John
Miss Hichens
Miss L. Hichens
Miss Usticke
2nd
Mrs Treweeke
Mrs Smith
Mrs Courtenay
Miss Treweeke
5th
Mrs John
Mrs Hill
Miss Guavas
6th
Mrs Cornish.

Subscribers.
GENTLEMEN.
Captn Wingrove
Mr Hoye
Mr Jno Borlase
Mr Stevenson jun.
Mr Saml John
Mr Wm Bolitho
Mr T. Giddy
Mr Rd Oxnam
Mr Wm Oxnam
2nd
Mr John
Mr Hill
Mr Smith
3rd
Mr Warne
Mr W. M. Hitchins
5th
Captn Roche
Mr H. Hichens
Mr Northmore
6th
Mr G. Woodis
7th
Revd Mr Borlase.

ABOVE: Penzance Assembly Book, 1791. (PMGL/WT) OPPOSITE: Mayor's Accounts 1706-7, with a reference to Carveth's usurpation of the Mayoralty. (CRO/WT)

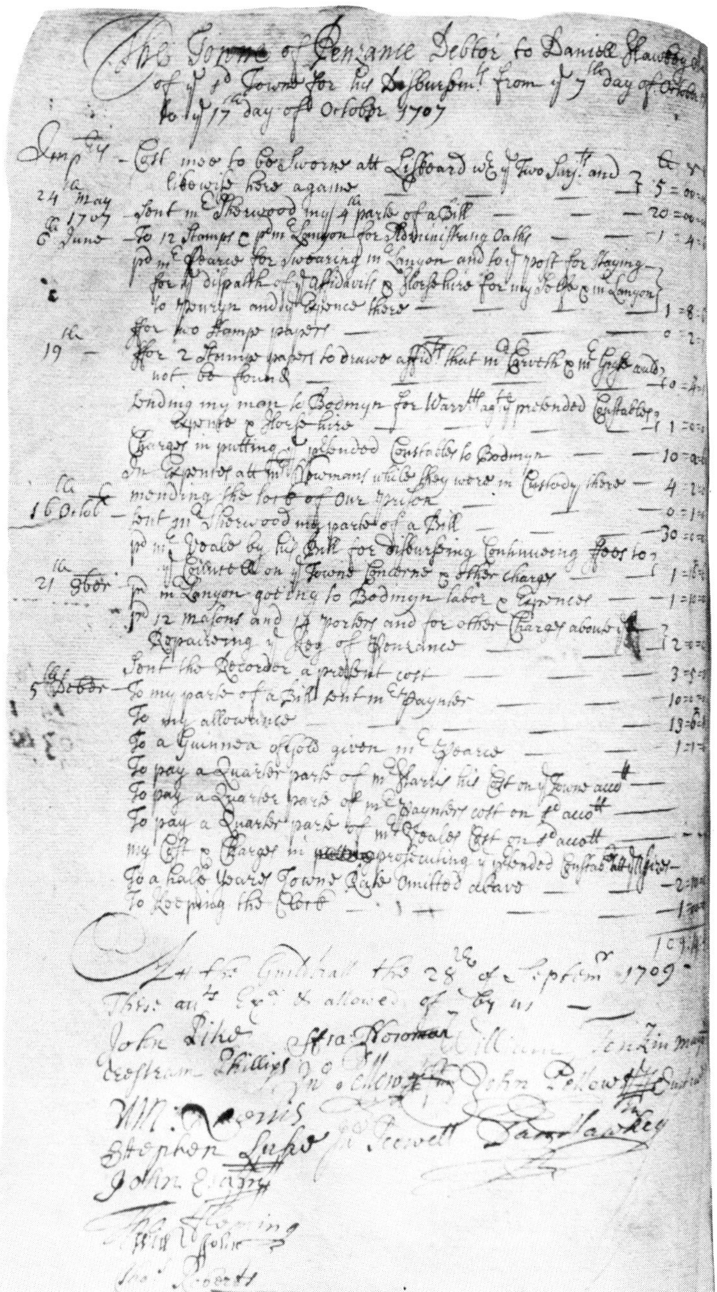

The Towne of Penzance Debtor to Daniell Hawkey ... of ye sd Towne for his Disbursemts from ye 7th day of October ... to ye 17th day of October 1707

Imps 4th	Cost mee to bee sworne att Liskeard wth ye two Justs and likewise here againe	5 = 00
24th May 1707	Sent Mr Sherwood my 1/4th parte of a Bill	20 = 00
6th June	To 12 Stamps & Mr Langon for Administring Oaths	1 = 4
	pd Mr Hoare for swearing Mr Langon and for post for staying for ye dispatch of ye Affidavits & Horse hire for my selfe & Mr Langon to Bodmyn and ye Expence there	1 = 8
	For two Stamps papers	0 = 2
19th	For 2 Stamps paper to drawe affidtt that Mr Carveth & Mr Griffith could not be found	0 = 4
	Sending my man to Bodmyn for Warrtt agt ye pretended Constables expence & Horse hire	1 = [illegible]
	Charges in putting ye pretended Constables to Bodmyn	10 = [illegible]
	On Expences att Mr Bowmans while they were in Custody there	4 = [illegible]
16th Octob	mending the lock of our Prison	0 = 1
	Sent Mr Sherwood my parte of a Bill	30 = [illegible]
	pd Mr Veale by his Bill for disbursing Continueing Fees to ye Counsell on ye Towns Concerns & other charges	1 = [illegible]
21 8bor	pd Mr Langon going to Bodmyn labor & Expences	1 = [illegible]
	pd 12 masons and 14 porters and for other Charges about Repairing ye Key of Penzance	2 = [illegible]
	Sent the Recorder a present cost	3 = [illegible]
5th 8ber	To my parte of a Bill sent Mr Paynter	10 = [illegible]
	To my allowance	13 = [illegible]
	To a Guinnea of Gold given Mr Hoare	1 = 1
	To pay a Quarter parte of Mr Harris his Cost on ye Towns acctt	
	To pay a Quarter parte of Mr Paynters cost on sd acctt	
	To pay a Quarter parte of Mr Veales Cost on sd acctt	
	My Cost & Charges in prosecuting ye pretended Constables ...	
	To a halfe yeare Towne Rent omitted above	2 = [illegible]
	To keeping the Clock	1 = [illegible]
		109 = [illegible]

Att the Guildhall the 28th of September 1709

This acctt Examd & allowed of by us

John Pike — Ricd Noman — William Jenkin mayor

Tristram Phillips — John ... — John Pellow

Wm Morris — Jo Pearce — Danll Hawkey

Stephen Lusk

John Evans

Thos Fleming

Will Usher

Thos Roberts

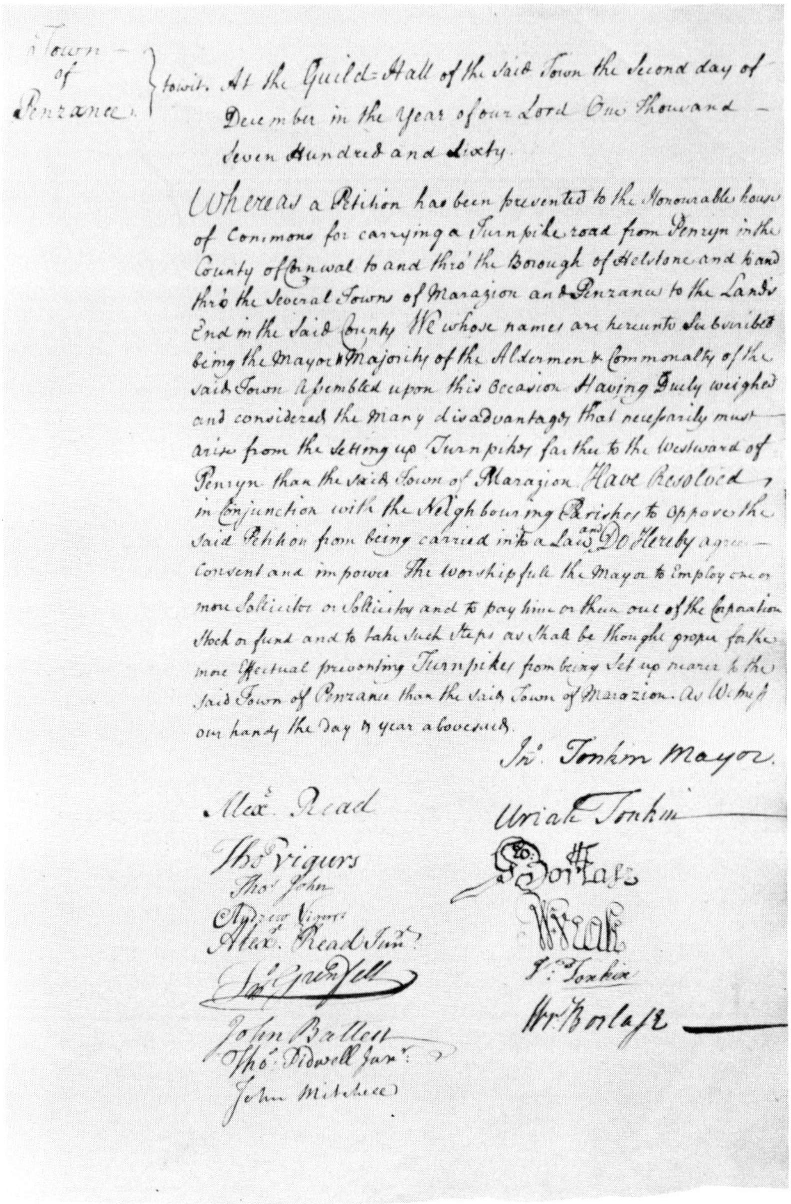
Town of Penzance } to wit. At the Guild-Hall of the said Town the Second day of December in the Year of our Lord One Thousand Seven Hundred and Sixty.

Whereas a Petition has been presented to the Honourable house of Commons for carrying a Turnpike road from Penryn in the County of Cornwal to and thro' the Borough of Helstone and to and thro' the several Towns of Marazion and Penzance to the Land's End in the said County We whose names are hereunto Subscribed being the Mayor & Majority of the Aldermen & Commonalty of the said Town Assembled upon this Occasion Having Duely weighed and considered the many disadvantages that necessarily must arise from the setting up Turnpikes farther to the Westward of Penryn than the said Town of Marazion Have Resolved in Conjunction with the Neighbouring Parishes to oppose the said Petition from being carried into a Law and Do Hereby agree Consent and impower The worshipfull the Mayor to Employ one or more Sollicitor or Sollicitors and to pay him or them out of the Corporation Stock or fund and to take such Steps as shall be thought proper for the more Effectual preventing Turnpikes from being Set up nearer to the said Town of Penzance than the said Town of Marazion. As Witness our hands the Day & year abovesaid.

Jno. Tonkin Mayor

Alexr. Read
Uriah Tonkin
Thos. Viguers
Jo. Borlase
Thos. John
Andrew Viguers
W. Veale
Alexr. Read Junr.
Jno. Grenfell
J. Tonkin
Wr. Borlase
John Ballett
Thos. Tidwell Junr.
John Mitchell

Objection to a new turnpike road being brought nearer to Penzance than Marazion, 1760. (CRO/WT)

The New Resort

Penzance during Napoleonic times was a most exciting place in which to live. The waters of Mount's Bay and the Channel beyond swarmed with British and enemy warships, skirmishes being frequent. Into its harbour sailed privateers escorting newly captured prizes, and naval vessels carrying dejected PoWs or the jubilant crews of retaken British ships. Revenue cutters, including the celebrated *Dolphin*, were constantly patrolling the coast on the look-out for smugglers who, in contemptuous disregard of the Continental blockade, continued to import illicit cargoes of wine and brandy. From time to time armed landing parties made forays through town and countryside, searching out reluctant young fishermen and farm labourers for impressment into His Majesty's Navy. By contrast, the Mount's Bay Volunteers drilled enthusiastically in readiness for an expected invasion that never materialised, winning high praise for their smartness and efficiency. Meanwhile, despite many alarms and excursions, life in Penzance went on much in its accustomed fashion. The markets and fairs were held at their appointed times, and Midsummer Eve bonfires blazed in its streets to the danger and delight of all inhabitants.

Some curious evidence of this is preserved in the details of a case (the King *v* Bromley) tried at the Cornwall Assizes, and reported in the *Sherborne Mercury* of 3 August 1812. The prosecutor was the Mayor of Penzance, and the traverser (defendant) one of a party who assembled on Midsummer Eve to light bonfires and hold the traditional celebrations. The local authorities always tended to be 'against' these fiery demonstrations on the grounds of public order and safety, and a constable, on the instructions of the Mayor, ordered them to disperse, but the merrymakers, 'thinking themselves justified by prescription', resisted the officer. The traverser was found guilty and sent up to the Court of King's Bench to receive sentence.

Small yet significant changes were taking place in the appearance of the town. At the beginning of the 19th century Market Jew Street looked very different. In place of the present array of shops along the Terrace there were a number of small houses, the only building of consequence the granite-fronted Poor House, built as an almshouse around 1660 by Francis Buller of Shillingham. The Terrace footpath was much wider, with a gradual slope instead of a wall in front, leaving only a narrow cartway on the southern side. In 1765 the Tonkin family, who occupied a house just above the entrance to Jennings' Lane, planted trees in the roadway from a point nearly opposite their residence to the old Market House. The Tonkins took a great pride in these trees, which formed a most attractive feature of the thoroughfare, and showed their proprietorial interest by frequently lopping and topping their branches. However, in 1805 the Corporation decided to remove the last two surviving trees to make what was described as 'an admirable improvement'. For Penzance then, as now, was beset by traffic, and beautiful as the trees were, it was felt expedient to sacrifice them. The Tonkin family, outraged by what they considered an act of official vandalism, brought an action against the Mayor at the County Assizes in August for the recovery of the value of the trees, but the jury, after a lengthy hearing, returned a verdict for the defendant.

It was during the early years of the 19th century that Penzance acquired the charming Regency terraces and squares which still form such a delightful feature of the town. North Parade was commenced in 1815 and completed in 1826. (South Parade had been built around 1790.) Between 1815 and 1820 the first part of Regent Terrace, together with Wellington Terrace and Place and houses at the rear and sides of North Parade, were erected. Marine Terrace was commenced in 1826. The following year saw Cornwall Terrace commenced and Clarence Street opened, though some years elapsed before the latter was finished. In 1829 Victoria Place was built and Morrab Place begun. Clarence Terrace was started in 1832, while Adelaide Street, commenced in 1828, was nearly completed in 1834, during which year Leskinnick Street and Terrace and Penwith Street were under construction. Penrose Terrace, started in 1835 and completed in 1839, which extended along the foot of Lescudjack Hill, was described by a contemporary as 'one of the best rows of houses in Penzance'. Regent Square, commenced in 1836, and elegant Regent Terrace, recommenced at the same time, were both completed around 1839.

Great wars produce unexpected side effects and the Napoleonic conflict brought at least one surprising benefit to Penzance. During the long years of that grim struggle most of the Continent was closed to British travellers; invalids and persons in delicate health were unable to escape the rigours of winter at such resorts as Nice or Genoa. They consequently sought out congenial places in their own country. One of the most favoured was Penzance, where the influence of the Gulf Stream, a southerly aspect and sheltered situation combined to produce a climate milder in winter and more equable in summer than anywhere else on mainland Britain. The great spate of building activity in the post-war period was a direct consequence of the town's development as a health resort.

With the advent of peace in 1814 there came a marked quickening of cultural activity. In that year was founded the Royal Geological Society of Cornwall, mainly through the efforts of Davies Gilbert (its first President), Dr J. Ayrton Paris, Rev Valentine Le Grice, Henry Boase, E. C. Giddy and others. The Penzance Library was established in 1818, and for a few years shared Geological House at North Parade with the senior institution. Both survive to this day.

This rather odd combination of health resort and cultural centre was strikingly reflected in Dr J. A. Paris's *Guide to the Mount's Bay* (1816), a work in which praise of the charms of the town is curiously mingled with much geological and scientific data. An enlarged second edition was called for in 1824, in which the author stated that, during the interim, the erection of commodious sea baths, the growing confidence of the public and medical profession in the superior mildness of the climate, and the general improvement in amenities of the place as a winter residence, had brought about a great increase in the number of invalids visiting this formerly obscure and comparatively neglected district.

Gradually, also, the advantages which Penzance possessed as a summer watering place began to be appreciated. The first residential accommodation provided specifically for holidaymakers appears to have been the Marine Hotel, built as a speculation in 1840. Described as near the sea in one of the greatest thoroughfares of the town, almost adjoining the public hot and cold water sea baths and the intended new Esplanade, it commanded extensive views of St Michael's Mount, the Bay and surrounding country. 'The want of a good House near the Sea, for the convenience of Invalids and others visiting Penzance during the Bathing Season, is too notorious to require further remark, and the present affords the opportunity to the man of business of forming one of the best establishments in the West of England.'

Penzance was remarkable for its number of industries. At Chyandour was one of the largest tanneries in Cornwall; two tin smelting works (Chyandour and Trereife) lay in its immediate vicinity, while in the town itself were four breweries, two wool combing establishments, and a wide variety of smaller factories and workshops. An alphabetical list of trades and employment in 1839 gives an excellent idea of the industries represented:

Bakers and confectioners, 29; basket makers, 14; block and pump makers, 5; bookbinders, 3; brewers, 17; blacksmiths and farriers, 33; carriers, 24; carvers and gilders, 1; coopers, 15; carpenters (house) and cabinet makers, 152; chandlers (tallow) 8; dyers, 2; farriers, 3; furriers, 1; glaziers, 1; hatters, 12; lime-burners, 6;

masons (including 9 granite cutters and 12 plasterers) 141; maltsters, 2; printers, 18; potters, 6; paper makers, 6; plumbers and braziers, 20; painters, 31; pipe makers, 2; rope makers, 8; shoemakers, 400 (this astonishing number is explained by the fact that many of the shoemakers also attended the weekly markets in neighbouring towns); saddlers, 20; statuary and stone masons, 4; shipwrights, 60; sailmakers, 10; tailors, 57; tanners, 40; tin smelters, 12; watchmakers and jewellers, 15; wheelwrights and coachmakers, 21; woolcombers and staplers, 15.

The town's population grew appreciably during the early part of the century, rising from 3,382 in 1801 to 5,224 in 1821 and 6,583 in 1831. The small chapel of St Mary's was no longer adequate and in 1825 its minister, Rev C. Valentine Le Grice, started a subscription for an enlarged church.

On 23 April 1828 a public meeting convened by Richard Edmonds, the chapel warden, resolved to rebuild the chapel on an enlarged scale; the foundation stone was laid on 17 August 1832 by the Mayor at the NW corner, not at the SE corner as is customary. The opening service took place on 25 November 1835. The Bishop of Exeter consecrated the new chapel on 30 August 1836.

The building was designed to take a congregation of 2,047, bringing the total accommodation of seats here and in the various nonconformist chapels to 6,487 for a population of 6,563, including children. The average number attending public worship on Sunday in 1836 was 2,845 in the morning and 3,125 in the evening.

The architect of the new St Mary's was Charles Hutchens of St Buryan, who had previously (1828) built a church at St Day which served as a prototype. Early Gothic Revival in style, it was one of a large group of churches built by Commissioners appointed by the Church Building Act of 1818 to meet the needs of developing towns. Its most notable feature is the Cornish tower which dominates every view of Penzance. Relics preserved from the old chapel include the door of the priests' vestry in Under Chapel Yard with the date 1672 on the arch; the small granite font now used as a holy water stoup; the alms box in the porch dated 1612; and the fine Tremenheeere memorial on the south wall dated 1701. The imposing high altar and canopy was erected in 1934 to commemorate the church's centenary. It was designed by architect R. F. Wheatly, FRIBA, and artist Ernest Proctor, ARA, and dedicated by Bishop Frere of Truro. After the spire of old St Mary's Chapel had been pulled down by ropes under the direction of John Semmens of Newlyn, the top stone with the vane was re-erected on the bell-tower of the Girls' National School. The vane, bearing the date 1789, was eventually restored to St Mary's, where it flashes in the sun atop the flagstaff 150 feet above street level.

A new district church of St Paul's, built as a proprietary chapel in 1843 in Clarence Street by Rev Henry Batten, who became its first minister, had a separate parish assigned to it in 1867. St Mary's, however, remained a chapel of ease until 1871 when, rather curiously, it obtained the gift of full rights so that its curate, who thereby became a vicar, might legally act in that capacity as a trustee of the new National School for Boys, opened in 1872. The Order in Council constituting the new parish was dated 24 March 1871. Prebendary Philip Hedgeland was the last Curate and first Vicar of St Mary's. The two parishes of St Mary and St Paul were united in 1973. In 1880 a new church of St John was built to serve the eastern part of the town, and a parish assigned to it two years later. In 1848 the parish of Newlyn was created out of Paul and Madron, the church of St Peter completed in 1866.

Some distance above St Mary's Church in Chapel Street stands the large Wesleyan Chapel, built in 1814, with a somewhat remarkable Italianate front. Chapel Street is not named after this building, as is sometimes supposed, but from the mediaeval St Mary's Chapel, as evidenced by its ancient name of Our Lady Street. The first Methodist chapel at Penzance, a small building near the South Parade, was opened in 1778; prior to this the Society held their meetings in a room behind a house in Market Jew Street, nearly opposite the former Congregationalist Chapel. By 1788 the membership had so greatly increased as to enable them to build a larger chapel in Queen Street, where they remained until their removal to the present Chapel Street building in 1814. The growth of population in the northern part of the town led the Methodists to open another chapel in St Clare Street in 1833.

The Society of Friends (Quakers) had a meeting place in the town as early as 1650, replaced by another one at Causewayhead in 1777. A Society of Congregationalists or Independents was also established at Penzance in the 17th century. The members met in a small chapel in Market Jew Street, built in 1707, which lasted until 1807, when it was replaced by a larger edifice on the same site.

In 1789 a body of Congregational Dissenters built a curious eight-sided chapel, known as the Octagon, near South Parade – its site is now occupied by the Government office block, Penlowarth. They shared this for some years with the Baptists but, on the Dissenters returning to the fold, the Baptists became sole occupiers of what they restyled the Jordan Chapel. From 1807-25 and 1843-63 its pastor was Rev George Charles ('Boatswain') Smith, known as the sailors' friend, one of the great social reformers of his age. Born in London in 1782 he was pressed for the Navy when still a boy, and served under Nelson at the Battle of Copenhagen (1803) on board the *Agamemnon*, earning a medal for bravery. Converted at Reading that same year, he trained for the ministry at Dock (Devonport), and his varied career included a mission to Wellington's army in Spain and France during 1813; but his real life's work began in London in 1819, where he opened the first Seamen's Floating Chapel, commenced open-air preaching (1822) for which he was often imprisoned, established the first Sailor's Home on the site of the Brunswick Theatre, which collapsed with much loss of life in 1828 - he himself directed the rescue operations – founded the first Temperance Society in Britain, and organised charitable institutions for the orphans of soldiers and sailors. He also laboured mightily to destroy the iniquitous crimping system by which sailors were lured or forced on board ships against their will. He ended his days in poverty at Penzance, a subscription having to be raised for his relief in his 81st year.

A group of seceders from the Baptist Society eventually moved to the Queen Street Methodist Chapel, which was then disused. Unity was soon re-established, but further dissension resulted in another split, the dissenters building the Clarence Street Baptist Chapel in 1836. Designed by Philip Sambell jun, of Truro, this was the first nonconformist chapel in Cornwall built in what was described as the 'proper ecclesiastical' (Anglo-Norman) style. St Mary's Roman Catholic Church in Rosevean Road was opened on 26 October 1843 with a Grand High Mass, a 'select Choir from Bath' taking part.

The *Official Guide to Penzance* (1876) lists further chapels, many of which are now defunct. They include the Bethel Chapel in Battery Square, at the Quay; the Bible Christian Chapel in Chapel Place, St Clare Street; Jews' Synagogue in New Street; the Methodist New Connexion Chapel in Abbey Street; the Plymouth Brethren Meeting Room in Alverton Street, opposite the Public Buildings, and the Primitive Methodist Chapel in Mount Street. Others were built later, such as the Free Methodist Chapel in Parade Street (1889), now an arts centre; the Richmond Methodist Church in Tolver Place (1907), and the New Connexion Chapel in Alexandra Road. The Salvation Army reopened the old Methodist Chapel in Queen Street in 1883 as their citadel.

The great Reform Bill of 1832 abolished the corrupt system of rotten boroughs which had become such a scandal in the parliamentary representation of the country. In similar fashion the Municipal Corporations Act of 1835 swept away the closed, self-perpetuating Corporations responsible for local government, replacing them with democratically elected bodies more in keeping with the spirit of the times. At Penzance, the new Corporation, consisting of 18 councillors and six aldermen, assumed office on 1 January 1836. It was dominated by men of progressive outlook, and carried out many desirable improvements to the harbour, water supply, drainage and other public facilities.

One of its first acts was to complete the task, initiated by its predecessor, of erecting a new Market House and Guildhall to replace the building put up on Richard Daniell's three-cornered plot in 1615. Designed by William Harris of Bristol, the foundation stone was laid on 11 July 1836. The completed building was opened just two years later, on 28 June 1838, the town being *en fete* for the occasion. With its pillared front, clock and dome, the Market House is perhaps the most imposing building in Penzance, but it has created an unfortunate bottleneck at the top of Market Jew Street. In 1845 a new fish market was opened in Princes Street to relieve the congestion caused by the 'standings' (stalls) set up all around the building by fisherwomen, farmers and others on market days.

With the old Market House also disappeared the notorious Penzance Borough Gaol or 'Black Hole', located at its eastern end adjoining the Corn Market, a dark, rat-infested, ill-ventilated room in which prisoners could scarcely stand upright and had only straw for bedding. This was almost certainly the place in which Mr Maxfield, the Methodist preacher, had been immured by Dr Walter Borlase in1745. The Corporation decided in 1826 to build a new prison on the western side of St Clare Street, complete with treadwheel and punishment room. Several convicted smugglers are recorded as among its involuntary inmates. The old Debtors' prison was in the stable yard of the picturesque Shoulder of Mutton Inn in the Greenmarket, offenders incarcerated within its gloomy confines being dependent on public charity for food and other necessities. This seems to have been little used after the close of the 18th century.

The year 1852 was a significant one in the annals of Penzance, as it saw the inauguration of the West Cornwall Railway between that town and Truro. This line was a successor to the old Hayle-Redruth railway opened in 1837 for mineral traffic and for regular passenger service in 1843. The West Cornwall Railway was opened between Penzance and Redruth on 11 March 1852 and for its entire length on 25 August; although the official ceremony was deferred to the latter date, the earlier occasion is in some ways more interesting, since it marked the first opportunity Penzance people had of enjoying this new mode of travelling.

On the morning of 28 February 1852 several directors were treated to a pre-opening ride over the new line. They travelled from Truro to Redruth by horse 'bus where, with invited guests, the party boarded a special train at 10.30 am. This consisted of five carriages, one of which was a handsome and luxurious first class coach of three compartments built in the Company's works at Carn Brea – 'the incipient Swindon of the West Cornwall line'. The engine was the appropriately nameed *Penzance*, also built at Carn Brea where, under the direction of Mr Brunton, engineer of the line, another powerful engine, the *Camborne*, was nearing completion – it still lacked wheels, owing to a strike, – to be followed by two others, the *Redruth* and the *Truro*.

The first stop was at Carn Brea to inspect the workshops; at Camborne, the train, until then running on rails laid upon stone blocks, got on to the new Barlow rails laid not on sleepers but by their own broad bearing directly on the road bed itself. At Angarrack viaduct a stop was made to allow this impressive 100 feet high wooden structure to be examined. At Hayle, they were received with cheers, then continued on past Treloweth smelting house and Wheal Darlington to 'Longbridge', where the train stopped to take up some directors and gentlemen who had walked out from Penzance to meet it. 'Having maintained a capital speed nearly the whole way from Hayle, it now dashed on over the level of Marazion Green to Chyandour, at the rate of about 30 miles an hour'. (*Royal Cornwall Gazette*.)

Direct railway communication with London and other parts of the country only became possible in 1859 with the opening of Brunel's Royal Albert Bridge across the Tamar, while the time-consuming 'break of gauge' at Truro, where the narrow gauge WCR met the broad gauge Cornwall Railway was not eliminated till 1867, by the laying of a 'third rail' between Truro and Penzance.

By the mid-19th century Penzance was large enough to provide its residents with a wide range of pleasures and entertainments. Each summer a circus visited the town, one being 'Hughes's Royal Mammoth Grand Oriental Equestrian Establishment', whose 'pavilion' was erected in John Hall's field, Alverton Lane, in June 1847. Alverton was also the venue of the annual Corpus Christi Fair, its attractions in 1841 including two rival theatres (Lawrence's and Hord's), Batty's menagerie, which boasted one of the finest collections of animals ever seen in Penzance and a waxworks featuring lifelike representations of the Queen and Prince Albert.

In 1857 Samuel Higgs jun, well known in Cornish and Australian mining circles, organised the first 'Penzance and Mount's Bay Regatta' as a replacement for Edwin Boyns' Mount's Bay and West of England horse races, temporarily suspended due to a new Government tax. The committee boat ss *Duke of Buccleugh* anchored off the Western Esplanade, where the Penzance Band discoursed sweet music to waiting thousands while the boats waited patiently for a breeze. The regatta proved highly successful, and became a feature of the Penzance summer scene. Residents of the harbour area, feeling rather left out in the cold by this event, in 1873 organised their own 'East End Regatta', which also ran for some years.

Penzance Swimming Matches, arranged by Penzance Swimming Association under the patronage of the Mayor and others, were first held in 1864, off the Queen's Hotel. Valuable prizes were offered, attracting first class swimmers from all over the West of England, and special excursion trains helped swell the numbers of spectators. But the most popular sport was cricket. Penzance Cricket Club was revived in 1853.

For young Penzance an eagerly anticipated occasion was the annual Band of Hope Gala. In 1865 thousands of children dressed in gay summer attire, and carrying colourful banners and flowers, formed a procession of such length that it took a quarter of an hour to pass any given spot. Headed by the Penzance Rifle Band, they marched through the town to the pleasant grounds of Trereife, where each boy and girl was supplied with tea, fruit and cakes, all afterwards joining in various games, 'the grassy slopes their ball-room and banquet hall, the beautiful spreading elms their shelter and shade, and a bright June sky their canopy'.

The Mount's Bay and West of England Races had been revived by 1865. The events that year included a race for ponies ridden by lads under sixteen years of age; the West of England Stakes; the Ladies' Plate for horses bred in either Devon or Cornwall and regularly hunted with packs of hounds – 'Gentlemen to ride in hunting-coats, breeches and boots' – and the Land's End and St Just in Penwith Stakes for horses owned by farmers or tradesmen in the county of Cornwall; all were flat races. There were also the Borough Stakes Hurdle Race, with heats about ¾ of a mile over six flights, and the Western Hunt Steeplechase for hunters across three miles of fair hunting country. It was said that 'the West Cornwall Railway, with its usual liberality', would 'convey and return all horses duly entered for the races, gratuitously, from Truro and all intermediate stations, and run extra and cheap trains for the accommodation of the public'.

Alongside these typically Victorian pleasures, the ancient traditional customs of the town – gathering shellfish from Larrigan Rocks at low tide on Shrove Tuesday; raffling for 'Lily-bangers' (gingerbread cakes) on Easter Monday; the excitement of Midsummer Eve bonfires and Quay Fair on the morrow, with a scaled down repeat on St Peter's Eve and Day (28-29 June); and 'curl' singing and 'guise' dancing at Christmas – continued to be observed with undiminished vigour. The practice of sounding 'May horns' (tin trumpets) by children to usher in the summer, increased to such an extent as to constitute a serious annoyance, which members of the Town Council solemnly debated at one of their meetings in 1865, when it was moved that 'May horns be put down – just in the way Midsummer fireworks are' – that is, nominally, and for appearance's sake only! It was not, indeed, until the 1930s that the authorities finally plucked up sufficient courage to ban the horns.

At somewhat rare intervals the Councillors themselves indulged in the good old custom of 'beating the Borough bounds'. In 1854, the Mayor (Richard Pearce) and Corporation assembled at the Green Market Cross, whence they proceeded to the western boundstone at Alverton, passing round the Borough limits to inspect other boundstones at Chapel St Clare and Chyandour. Taking to the water at the Albert Pier, the 'beaters' followed a seaward course marked by buoys to visit the last boundstone at Wherrytown. Various ancient practices were observed on the way, the Corporation also receiving the hospitality of several gentlemen over whose lands they passed, the pleasures of the day concluding with a five o'clock dinner at the Union Hotel.

On 10 April 1860 a new Borough Fire Brigade was formed, with John Matthews (Borough Surveyor) as Superintendent, John Olds (1st Captain), W. H. Wallis (2nd Captain) and W. Cliff (3rd Captain). There were also two turncocks and nine firemen. Its regulations decreed that in the event of a fire, information should be given at the watch-house, so that the fire-bell might be rung by the policeman on duty. Should no policeman be available, the alarm could be given by pulling the bell rope in a cupboard over the fireplace. If required, working men could be employed to work the engines, being given pay tickets for their services. It was further ordered that the First Cornwall Rifle Volunteers were to form a line around the fire, to keep order and protect life and property, and to render any assistance required by the Superintendent. Two years later a uniform was provided for the firemen, consisting of a scarlet woollen loose tunic with a dark blue belt, the helmet being 'a superior kind of hard miner's hat'.

During the mid-19th century Penzance Corporation made strenuous efforts to improve the town's water supply. A watercourse had been constructed to connect Madron Well with a reservoir under the present cattle market, at the top of Causewayhead in the 1750s, but much of Penzance still had to depend on wells and other private sources. In 1852, after various difficulties had been overcome, virtually the whole town was furnished with an excellent water supply from the Brick Kiln Moor stream via a new reservoir at Polteggan on land owned by H. L. Stephens of Tregenna Castle, St Ives. This was supplemented eight years later by a second, larger reservoir on land adjacent to the existing basin bought of Gen Tremenheere for £400. The two reservoirs were united on 10 October 1860 during a ceremony attended by the Mayor and entire Corporation. They processed in thick rain – doubtless considered a good augury – to Hendra Gate to inspect one of their chief sources of water supply and thence to Polteggan mill-leat to view the two reservoirs attractively sited just under the entrance to Trengwainton. Between them, on Trengwainton slope, a tent was pitched, where the Mayor, Francis Boase Esq welcomed the visitors to luncheon. His Worship then turned on water into the new reservoir, which he christened 'The Duke of Cornwall', the other being already distinguished by the name of the Queen. Various healths were thereupon drunk, including those of Sam Higgs, Secretary of the Waterworks and Sewerage Committee, and John Matthews, the indefatigable Borough Engineer. In 1854 the municipal authorities selected a site on the Glebe land at Alverton, and two years later the Geological Society joined the scheme by deciding to erect new premises on the same ground. Unfortunately, difficulties arose in obtaining land from the Ecclesiastical Commissioners, and the project was temporarily shelved. A local landowner subsequently acquired an interest in the Glebe, and protracted negotiations resulted in the final site being too small and too near the road to permit the imposing setting envisaged.

Plans for the Public Buildings were prepared by John Matthews, Borough Surveyor, and Messrs Olver & Son, of Falmouth were appointed contractors. The foundation stone was laid on 27 April 1864, and the opening ceremony was on 10-11 September 1867. Fashioned in Lamorna granite, the edifice has a dignified though rather heavy appearance, and admirably reflects the civic pride of the men of mid-Victorian Penzance. It consists of a central main hall, known as St John's Hall, used for concerts and other public events, a west wing occupied by the Geological Society, and an east wing which in 1867 contained the Guildhall, the Penzance Library, Chess Club, Natural History Society's Museum, Mount Sinai Lodge of Freemasons, Police Station, and various offices. It had been intended also to accommodate the County Court in the building but, as the legal authorities required preferential use of the Guildhall over the Corporation, this idea was dropped at the sacrifice of a £1,500 contribution from the Treasury.

Celebrations to mark the opening were arranged on a lavish scale, their most interesting feature being an historic lifeboat race, in which six West Cornwall boats participated, the winner, after a stern contest, being the *Cousins William and Mary Ann of Bideford*, from Sennen. Other events included a public dinner in the Geological Society's rooms; a concert by the Choral Society in St John's Hall, assisted by an orchestra and the splendid organ, a dinner to the poor in the Corn Exchange, where seven hundredweight of beef, 45 puddings of seven pounds each and large quantitites of ale were consumed; a 'treat' for 2,000 children consisting of a 'perambulation' of the streets in the rain, addresses from various clergymen and a fourpenny bun apiece, a firework display; and the ascent of a fire balloon from the buildings with fireworks attached, which emitted brilliant colours as it rose high above the town and floated away towards Castle-an-Dinas.

Several Royal visits took place during the 19th century, including the famous occasion when Queen Victoria, Prince Albert and the Princess Royal lingered in Mount's Bay for two days – 5 and 6 September 1846 – during the course of a Channel cruise. The Prince landed at Penzance and made a tour of the town, while on the following day the Queen and he visited St Michael's Mount and inspected the castle. On 25 July 1865 the Prince and Princess of Wales (later Edward VII and Queen Alexandra) landed at the Mount, made a descent of the famous submarine mine at Botallack, and opened the new thoroughfare at Penzance which still bears the Princess's name. These events have been much written about in various histories, but one Royal visit which has gone completely unnoticed is that of the Queen of the Netherlands on 5 March 1874. Arriving by train from Torquay, she was welcomed by the Mayor N. B. Downing, and Town Clerk, E. H. Rodd, after which the Royal party drove in two carriages and pairs to the Logan Rock at Castle Treryn. The rock having been duly 'logged' and her Majesty having admired the beautiful stretch of coastline extending towards Porthcurno, the journey was resumed to its ultimate goal, Land's End. She then returned to the appropriately named Queen's Hotel at Penzance for lunch, and was later seen off at the station by Mr and Mrs T. S. Bolitho and many hundreds of spectators.

In 1870 parts of an old workhouse and prison in St Clare Street, including the garden and yard outside the prison walls, treadwheel sheds and cells, were purchased as a site for the Penzance Infirmary. This institution had its origins in the Penzance Public Dispensary and Humane Society, formed in 1809 with premises on the Terrace in Market Jew Street. In 1813 it moved to a building in Chapel Street near the Vicarage, and later occupied Baines House next to the Methodist Chapel in the same street. The Infirmary at St Clare opened in 1874 and has since been extensively rebuilt and enlarged. It is now the principal hospital for all West Cornwall.

18 July 1878 saw the birth of *The Cornishman* newspaper. Its first editor was Albert Charles Wildman, who had previously edited the *Cornish Telegraph*, established at Penzance in 1851. Subsequent editors of *The Cornishman* have included Herbert Thomas, Hoole Jackson, Jas L. Palmer and John Page.

In 1879 work began on replacing the puny railway station of 1852 with the present imposing terminus, described at the time of its opening on 18 November as 'one of the finest stations west of London'. It was designed by Lancaster Owen, head of the Construction Department of the Great Western Railway and the contractors were Messrs Vernon & Ewens, of Cheltenham, who were also responsible for the old stations at North Road and Millbay (Plymouth) and Torquay. The lofty roof, with its span of 80 feet and length of nearly 250 feet, forms the most striking feature of the building; including the lantern, about one-third is glazed. In the early days there was a boiler house in one of the platform recesses for filling footwarmers. The station's width was sufficient to accommodate three broad gauge or four narrow gauge lines of rails.

On 7 October 1880 occurred the great Mount's Bay Storm, which caused much havoc both on sea and land. The Mousehole fishing boat *Jane* was broken to pieces amidst tremendous seas while running for shelter in Penzance harbour, all seven members of her crew being drowned; in addition, no less than thirty other Mount's Bay fishing vessels, mostly belonging to Newlyn and Mousehole, were sunk and destroyed at their moorings. The Western Esplanade and Wherrytown suffered severely, and the road between Larrigan and Newlyn was washed away.

1880 saw the opening of the School of Art in Morrab Road and the Arcade near the top of Market Jew Street. The Post Office in Market Jew Street, built by a Mr Berry to the design of James Hicks of Redruth, was completed in November 1883. At its opening, T. S. Bolitho gave some fascinating reminiscences of the postal service at Penzance during the previous hundred years. In 1785 a mail coach was established as far west as Plymouth, its route later extended to Falmouth. [William Birch of Stoke Damarel instigated this service — the publisher is his direct descendant — *Ed.*]. For some time after that the mail was carried on horseback from Penzance to Falmouth; but in 1808 'some sort of carriage' – actually John 'Dadda' Thomas's *Royal Kitereen*, named after his wife, Kitty – performed this duty. On its withdrawal, a horseman, Pascoe, again took over. The mail from St Ives was carried by an old woman – Jenny Brewer – in a basket.

There was then a daily postal service, letters posted in London on Monday being delivered at Penzance on Thursday. Mr Bolitho's brother Edward could remember a man going through the village of Chyandour crying out the news of the battle and burning of Moscow (1812). He himself recollected a man riding in shouting 'Great news, good news!' and his father, on opening his post bag found in it the *Courier* with details of 'a glorious victory' at Waterloo. That battle was fought on a Sunday, but news of it did not reach Penzance till the following Sunday.

At that time letters were delivered in Penzance by a woman who carried a basket. (This was little Betty Williams, who could not read, yet never failed to bring them to the right people.) Later a man used to go round with a bell and collect letters from street to street. In 1818 the Post Office was located in Alverton opposite the entrance to Clarence Street, being kept by a Mr Fleming. It was then transferred to Chapel Street, first under Mr Phillips, and then by a famous local character, 'kind-hearted if sharp-tongued' Miss Swain. On her retirement in 1864 the office was removed to the Market House basement, J. G. Uren becoming Postmaster, and he it was who effected the final transfer to the present premises.

A valuable addition to the amenities of Penzance was made in 1888 when the Corporation purchased Morrab House and three acres of adjoining fields for £3,120; in the amazingly short space of just over a year the fields were transformed by Reginald Upcher, a London landscape gardener, into attractive subtropical gardens. Morrab House itself was built in 1841 by Samuel Pidwell, also a Londoner, who came to Cornwall for health reasons and died at Penzance in 1854. A man of many interests, he climbed Mont Blanc in 1837, was a member of the Royal Yacht Club, set up a brewery at Penzance, became the town's Mayor in 1844 and 1849, and served as Secretary of the Royal Geological Society of Cornwall. In 1889 Morrab House became the permanent home of the Penzance Library which, because of its lovely setting, was once referred to by Sir Arthur Quiller Couch as 'a library in a garden'. It is today one of the few subscription libraries remaining in the country, richly stored with many literary treasures acquired during its more than 160 years' existence.

1893 saw the opening, on 7 July, of the Princess May recreation grounds at Treneere, now the venue of the Corpus Christi fair, and of the Free Library in Morrab Road on 13 October. In 1895 the Passmore Edwards Art Gallery at Tolcarne was erected as a memorial to the great Cornish painter, John Opie; it also symbolised the growing importance of the Newlyn school of artists established around 15 or 20 years earlier. Newlyn attracted widespread notice again the following year, when riots broke out in May between East Coast and Cornish fishermen on the vexed question of Sunday fishing.

On 23-24 May 1899 Penzance played host to the county's own regiment, the 2nd Battalion of the Duke of Cornwall's Light Infantry. The battalion, which had previously visited Camborne, Hayle, Lelant and St Ives, marched to Penzance by the 'old road' through Halsetown, Cripples' Ease and Gulval. On the following day the ceremony of trooping the colours was carried out at Castle Horneck by HMS *Leda*, the first CRGA, 2nd Batt DCLI and A Co 1st VBDCLI.

OPPOSITE ABOVE: *The Brilliant* horse omnibus passing old Ponsandane House, Penzance, 1843, and BELOW: Stage coach at the Union Hotel, Chapel Street, Penzance

UNION HOTEL

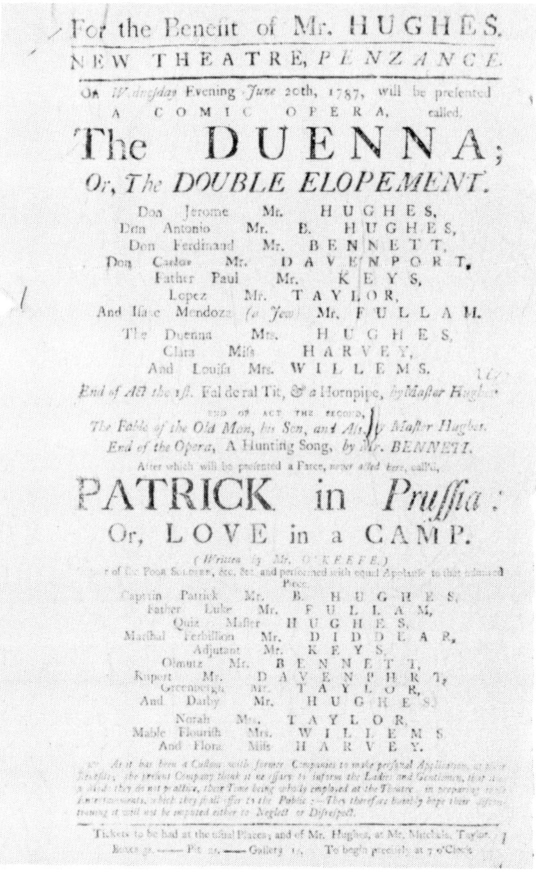

For the Benefit of Mr. HUGHES.
NEW THEATRE, *PENZANCE.*

On *Wednesday* Evening *June* 20th, 1787, will be presented
A COMIC OPERA, called,

The DUENNA;
Or, The DOUBLE ELOPEMENT.

Don Jerome Mr. HUGHES,
Don Antonio Mr. B. HUGHES,
Don Ferdinand Mr. BENNETT,
Don Carlos Mr. DAVENPORT,
Father Paul Mr. KEYS,
Lopez Mr. TAYLOR,
And Isaac Mendoza (*a Jew*) Mr. FULLAM.
The Duenna Mrs. HUGHES,
Clara Miss HARVEY,
And Louisa Mrs. WILLEMS.

End of Act the 1st. Fal de ral Tit, & a Hornpipe, *by Master Hughes.*
END OF ACT THE SECOND,
The Fable of the Old Man, his Son, and Ass, by Master Hughes.
End of the Opera, A Hunting Song, *by Mr. BENNETT.*
After which will be presented a Farce, *never acted here,* call'd,

PATRICK in *Prussia*:
Or, LOVE in a CAMP.

(*Written by Mr. O'KEEFE,*)
[illegible] of the POOR SOLDIER, &c. &c. and performed with equal Applause to that admired Piece.

Captain Patrick Mr. B. HUGHES,
Father Luke Mr. FULLAM,
Quiz Master HUGHES,
Marshal Ferbillion Mr. DIDDEAR,
Adjutant Mr. KEYS,
Olmutz Mr. BENNETT,
Rupert Mr. DAVENPORT,
Greenberg Mr. TAYLOR,
And Darby Mr. HUGHES.
Norah Mrs. TAYLOR,
Mable Flourish Mrs. WILLEMS,
And Flora Miss HARVEY.

As it has been a Custom with former Companies to make personal Application at private Families, the present Company think it necessary to inform the Ladies and Gentlemen, that [illegible] *they do not practise, their Time being wholly employed at the Theatre, in preparing* [illegible] *Entertainments, which they shall offer to the Public;—They therefore humbly hope their* [illegible] *it will not be imputed either to Neglect or Disrespect.*

Tickets to be had at the usual Places; and of Mr. Hughes, at Mr. Michael's, Taylor.
Boxes [illegible] —— Pit [illegible] —— Gallery [illegible] To begin precisely at 7 o'Clock.

ABOVE: Royal Mail vans and horse omnibuses outside the First and Last inn at Penzance. BELOW: 1787 Playbill. (PMGL/WT)

LEFT: Sir Humphry Davy. (PHM) RIGHT: Davies Gilbert, formerly Giddy, 1767-1839. Assumed his wife's name of Gilbert in 1817. BELOW: The Brontë sisters, painted by their brother Branwell. (NPG)

Old Workhouse and Prison Premises, Penzance, for Sale.

TO be SOLD by AUCTION, (under the sanction of the Lords Commissioners of Her Majesty's Treasury,) at the 'WESTERN HOTEL,' Penzance, on Wednesday, the 20th of March inst., at 3 o'clock in the afternoon, in one or more lots, and subject to such conditions as may be determined on at the time of sale, by Mr. A. BERRYMAN, for the remainder of an absolute Term of 100 years from 24th June, 1824, and subject to a conventionary rent of £10 per annum, all those BUILDINGS and PREMISES at ST. CLARE STREET, in the Borough of Penzance, formerly used and occupied as the

WORKHOUSE

of the said Borough, and also all those other Buildings and Premises recently used as the

PRISON

of the said Borough, together with the Courtlage and Garden lying between such buildings respectively; containing about 34 laces of Ground.

The whole Premises are in one enclosure, measuring 206 feet in length from North to South, and 138 feet in width at the Northern end, and 106 feet in width at the Southern end, and are the Property of the Mayor, Aldermen, and Burgesses of the said Borough of Penzance.

The Buildings are substantial and in good order, and capable, at a comparatively small outlay, of being converted into Dwellings.

For viewing the Premises apply to Mr. OLDS, Superintendent of Police, at No. 28, St. Clare-street, and for further particulars to the Auctioneer, or at the Offices of

E. H. RODD,
Town Clerk.

Penzance, March 1st, 1867.

N. HOLMAN AND SONS,

AGRICULTURAL IMPLEMENT MAKERS AND GENERAL IRONFOUNDERS, PENZANCE,

BEG to announce to their friends and customers that they have MADE A CONSIDERABLE REDUCTION in the price of many articles comprised in their extensive stock, and would direct attention to such as are more particularly adapted to the present season.

P R I C E S.

Improved portable thrashing machines......		£27 10 0
Three-horse power ditto ditto.........		23 0 0
Two-horse power ditto ditto.........		18 0 0
One-horse power ditto ditto.........		15 0 0
Winnowing machines, from	£6 10 0 to	8 0 0
Steaming apparatuses, from	£5 10 0 to	8 0 0
Arish rakes, adapted for raking Pilf, with lever, from................	£3 5 0 to	6 10 0
Improved cultivator, with acting lever from	£5 10 0 to	7 10 0
Tormentors of every description, from	£2 15 0 to	5 10 0
Manure drills of all descriptions, from	£4 0 0 to	6 10 0
Root graters, from	£3 5 0 to	4 10 0
Grass seed drills..............................		3 10 0
Seed drills, for sowing mangold, carrots, or turnips.....................................		1 17 6
Ditto, for sowing turnips only		1 8 0
Gardner's turnip-cutters.........	£4 10 0 to	5 10 0
Horse hoes, with banking gruters...........		2 10 0
Horse hoes and bankers light		1 17 6
Revolving slicers, from.......	£2 10 0 to	4 0 0
Ploughs of every description,	£2 5 0 to	4 4 0
Improved chaff-cutters, from..	£2 10 0 to	9 0 0
Revolving pigs'-troughs' from	10s to	1 0 0
Iron harrow's (each)		1 5 0
Chain harrows, from	£3 5 0 to	5 5 0

N.B. A Stock of Slabs, Ovens, Launders, Ships' Windlasses, Winches, &c., constantly on Sale.

AGENTS FOR THE SALE OF

THE MACHINES AND IMPLEMENTS OF B. SAMUELSON, BANBURY; AND PICKSLEY, SIMS, AND CO., BEDFORD FOUNDRY, LANCASHIRE.

ALL ARTICLES SUPPLIED AT LIST PRICES.

A Stock of Super Phosphate, &c., always on hand.

Their

PORTABLE THRASHING MACHINE

(so generally and highly approved at all local exhibitions) and capable of thrashing 50 bushels a day,

CAN NOW BE HAD ON HIRE AT 10s. PER DAY.

(With engineer 15s. a day.)

LEFT: The Workhouse was sold in 1867. RIGHT: Penzance Market House in the 1890s. (RCL) BELOW: Holmans advertise in 1860.

1865. 1865.

Mount's Bay and West of England Races.

PENZANCE, FRIDAY, 28TH OF JULY, 1865.

PROGRAMME.

A PONY RACE: A FLAT RACE FOR PONIES not exceeding 13 hands high, for £5, added to a Sweepstakes of 5s each, second horse to save his stakes; to be ridden by boys under 16 years of age, in colours; four to start or no race.

WEST OF ENGLAND STAKES: A FLAT RACE of 5 sovereigns each, with £60 added, whole forfeit, for all ages; 2 years old 6 st., 3 yrs. 8 st. 7 lbs., 4 yrs. 9 st. 7 lbs., 5 yrs. 10 st., 6 yrs. and aged 11 st.; winners 7 lbs. extra—mares and geldings allowed 3 lbs. and all horses trained in Cornwall or Devon 7 lbs. Second horse to save his stake, and the winner to pay £5 towards expenses. Heats about one mile and half.

THE LADIES' PLATE: A FLAT RACE of 20s each, with £20 added, for horses that have been bred in either of the Counties of Cornwall or Devon, and regularly hunted with an established pack of hounds. Gentlemen to ride in hunting-coats, breeches, and boots—to carry 11 st. 7 lbs.—winners 7 lbs. extra. The 2nd horse to receive £3 from the stakes and the 3rd horse to save his stake. The winner to pay two guineas towards expenses. Heats about a mile and a half. Five horses to start or the public money will not be added.

THE LAND'S-END AND ST. JUST IN PENWITH STAKES: A FLAT RACE for horses the property of farmers or tradesmen in the County of Cornwall, for £10 with 10s each. The same course as the West of England stakes. 3 yrs. old 7 st., 4 yrs. 7 st. 7 lbs., 5 yrs. 8 st., 6 yrs. and aged 9 st. 10 lbs. The second horse to save his stake.

THE BOROUGH STAKES: A HURDLE RACE; heats about ¾ of a mile over 6 flights, for £35, added to a sweepstakes of 20s—whole forfeit. The owner of the second horse to receive £2 from the stakes, and that of the third horse to save his stake; the winner to pay £3 towards expenses. Five horses to start or the public money will not be added. Weights same as Western Hunt stakes.

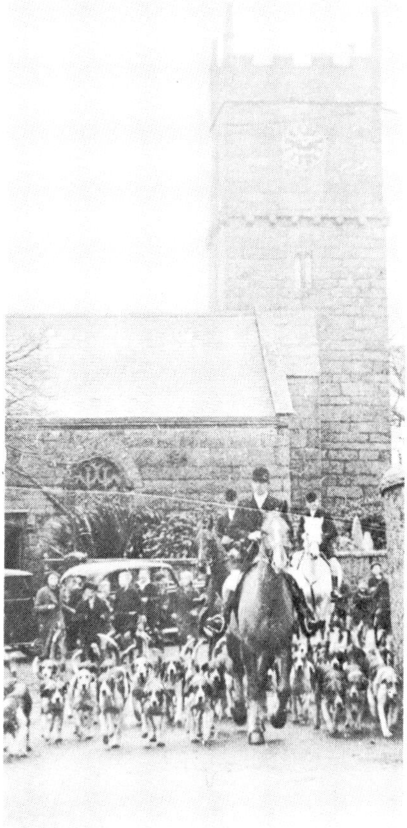

LEFT: Part of the Mount's Bay and West of England races programme. RIGHT: The annual meet at Madron; Lt Col E. H. Bolitho, Lord Lieutenant of Cornwall, leads on horseback. (PHM/JJC) BELOW: Penzance v Civil Service cricket match, played at Poltair 17-19 August 1866. (PMGL)

ABOVE: Penzance Borough steam fire engine presented by R. F. Bolitho of Ponsandane in 1895. BELOW: St Mary's Chapel, Penzance, drawn on 25 July 1832, shortly before its demolition. (RIC) OPPOSITE ABOVE: Bathing machine on the Promenade beach. CENTRE: The old Market House, taken down in the 1830s. (RCL) BELOW: Advertisement for the Queen's Hotel from *The Official guide to Penzance* 1876. Built in 1861 and enlarged in 1871 and 1908.

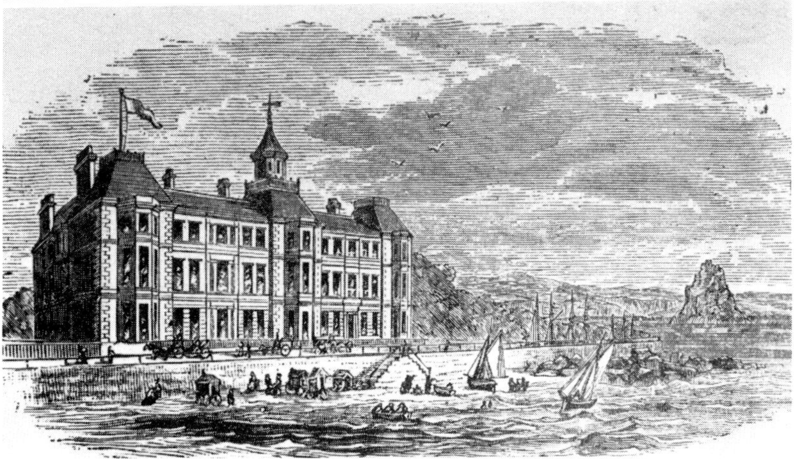

ABOVE: Market Jew Street c1893. Gibson's photographic studio on the left, with flag flying. (RIC/G) BELOW: The Serpentine factory, which was taken down for the Bedford Bolitho Gardens.

ABOVE: Baths taken down in 1883. (RIC/G) BELOW: A rare sight – frozen pond in the MorrabGardens, 1895. (RIC)

ABOVE: Neddy Betty's Lane, c1830, when gas lighting was first introduced into Penzance. The name derived from an old thatched inn at its eastern corner kept by Edward Betty. This was changed to Albert Street after the Prince Consort visited the town in 1846. (RIC/G – presumably from a painting.) BELOW: Penzance in 1817. (RCL)

ABOVE: Penzance from Gulval, by J. T. Blight c1850. (RCL) BELOW: Gulval parish church in its beautiful sylvan setting. (PHM)

ABOVE: The Old Inn c1885. The gentleman on horseback is Mr Polglase. (PHM/G) BELOW: Old buildings near Sutton's seeds establishment. (DM)

ABOVE: Mrs Eddy, Benjamin Corin and Amelia Ann Corin, in front of their cottage, demolished in 1894 when a wall was built around the churchyard. (DM) BELOW: Nineteenth century tranquillity at Gulval (RIC/G)

ABOVE: Hawke's Farm, 1899. Viscount Exmouth spent his boyhood days here. (RCL) BELOW: The Market Cross, 1829. (PHM)

ABOVE: Market Cross being removed from the bottom of Causewayhead in 1899 prior to its re-erection at the western end of the Market House where it remained until 1925. (PMGL) BELOW: Mousehole, 1910 (RCL)

ABOVE: Penzance railway station, 1870, showing the third rail for mixed gauge working. (PHM/G) BELOW: The locomotive *Penzance* photographed in the town.

Times of Change

One of the more pleasant events associated with the opening years of the present century was a return visit paid by Edward VII to Penzance and St Michael's Mount on 9 April 1902, 37 years after his visit as Prince of Wales in 1865. The King landed from the Royal yacht at Marazion in Lord St Levan's barge and drove to Penzance. After driving through Penzance his Majesty returned to Marazion and crossed to St Michael's Mount where he took tea with the proprietor.

On 17 July 1903 the Alexandra Grounds on the Promenade were opened by the Mayoress, Mrs J. Vivian Thomas, on land given by Mrs T. Robins Bolitho, of Trengwainton, so adding another to those valuable open spaces which help to give many parts of the town such an attractive 'green' character. A link with the past was severed in October 1906 by the demolition of the Coinage Hall or Triangular Cellars erected in 1816 near the quay. The Penzance County School for Boys – later renamed the Humphry Davy school in honour of Penzance's greatest son, and now a sixth form college – was erected at Treneere in 1909.

A somewhat remarkable 'non-event' took place between 20-24 July 1910, when nearly 200 warships assembled in Mount's Bay under Admiral Sir William May, as Commander-in-Chief, for an intended great ceremonial review by King George V, Queen Mary, Princess Mary and Prince George. This mighty armada, the largest ever brought together in western waters, included all the ships of the Home, Mediterranean and Channel Fleets, comprising 27 battleships, 37 cruisers, 67 destroyers, 24 torpedo boats, 25 submarines and 15 other craft, ranged in nine long lines filling the whole of Mount's Bay from St Michael's Mount to Mousehole. The submarines were placed abreast of the Promenade; beyond them stretched the destroyers, and outside these lay the cruisers and dreadnoughts. It was planned that the warships should undertake a number of evolutions; but on the 24th a strong WSW by SW wind, with heavy seas, obliged them to weigh anchor and proceed to Torbay. The weather was so bad that several of the giant battleships broke out their anchors and were dragging astern, with the choice of fouling a neighbour or bringing up on a lee shore, when the signal came to leave Mount's Bay. Mr Grahame-White, the 'intrepid aeronaut', thrilled spectators on shore by flying over the fleet in his aeroplane before their departure.

Mount's Bay witnessed the intrusion of some genuine flesh-and-blood as opposed to steel leviathans on 1 July 1911 – a school of about 60 bottle-nosed whales which became stranded on the sands when their leader, the bull whale, apparently made an error of navigation. Sad to say, many barbarities were committed upon the helpless creatures, some – the lucky ones – being shot, and others mutilated while still alive by souvenir hunters. Forty managed to get away on the returning tide, but they seemed completely disorientated, being without their leader.

In May 1912 electric light was first introduced into the town, while on 12 June Chyandour tin smelting works was closed after nearly 200 years. Another sign of the times was the opening of the Picture Theatre cinema at Causewayhead on 29 November. Penzance County School for Girls opened on 23 September and the new lifeboat house at Penlee, with a deep water slipway, on 25 October 1913.

With the outbreak of war in August 1914 Penzance harbour resumed the role it had played so well during the Napoleonic period. A naval base was established there, and between February 1915 and 15 March 1919, 10,585 vessels carrying 17,000,000 tons of cargo were escorted in convoy from Mount's Bay to France. Thirty five of these ships were lost, 582 lives saved by escorting vessels, while patrolling vessels saved nearly 4,000 more. The Penzance patrol salvaged 28 ships. About 70 vessels were employed at the base, and the personnel comprised 1,200 officers and men.

1915 saw the closing of the Penzance Wesleyan Day Schools and the opening (on 8 February) of Lescudjack Council Schools (now the Mount's Bay Comprehensive). On 24 May 1916 the Bedford Bolitho Gardens were opened on the site of the old Serpentine Works at Wherrytown, and the Richard Bolitho Gardens on Newlyn Green as Penzance's Tercentenary Memorial. During October of that year an ancient bronze cannon, thought to be a relic of the Armada, found at Low Lee, was presented to the town and placed in front of the Public Library in Morrab Road, where it may still be seen.

Peace was celebrated on 19 July 1919 with a civic procession, a children's entertainment and dancing on the Promenade, but the economic depression which followed soon after brought a different mood. In February 1920 a thousand St Just and Pendeen miners and clay workers marched to Penzance to protest against the high price of butter – then 5s per lb – and overturned cans of milk into the harbour. On 14 May 1922 the Penzance War Memorial was unveiled on the site of the old 18th century battery, a dignified obelisk which forms a prominent landmark near the eastern end of the Promenade. In 1924 the Alexandra Bowling Green and Tennis Courts were acquired by the Corporation. Lloyds' Bank was established in the Market House on the site of the former Corn Exchange during the following year, while that well known pleasure centre on the Promenade, the Winter Gardens, opened during November 1926. A notable event in 1928 was the revival of the Cornish Gorsedd at Boscawen-un on 21 September, while on 23 June 1929 another ancient custom, that of lighting traditional Midsummer Eve bonfires on hilltops throughout the county, was revived, both these events signifying the growing influence of the Old Cornwall movement, whose first Society (at St Ives) had been founded in 1920.

An important change in local government administration occurred in 1934 with the enlargement of the borough boundary to take in most of the parish of Paul (including Newlyn, Mousehole, and Churchtown at the top of the hill), a part of Madron (with Heamoor and Tolcarne) and part of Gulval (including Churchtown). The Council itself was also enlarged to give effective representation to the increased population it now served, the district being divided into four electoral wards represented by eight aldermen and 24 councillors. A new coat of arms was obtained, replacing, not before time, the repellent and nonsensical device of St John the Baptist's head by a shield incorporating symbols representing all parts of the enlarged Borough, flanked by (as supporters) a pirate (an allusion to the Gilbert and Sullivan opera *The Pirates of Penzance*) and a fisherman.

One of the new Council's first achievements was the completion of the Bathing Pool by the Battery Rocks in 1935. It also greatly stepped up the municipal housing programme initiated by its predecessor. Many dilapidated properties were demolished and new, large housing estates created on the town's outskirts in a welcome and necessary programme of regeneration.

The inter-war years showed a steady increase in the tourist industry. Though lacking the golden beaches and picture postcard charm of some neighbouring resorts, Penzance had much to offer the holidaymaker – good leisure and sports facilities, beautiful sub-tropical gardens and a fine promenade, while the development of a comprehensive motor 'bus service, replacing the horse brakes of an earlier day, enhanced its value as a centre for exploring the whole Penwith area. Most visitors still arrived by train; as yet, only a modest trickle of cars filtered through the green lanes of the county, harbingers of the flood that was to follow in the '60s and '70s.

The Second World War brought horror and destruction to Penzance in a way it had not experienced since the Spanish raid 350 years before. Edgar Rees, in *Old Penzance*, gives the following grim statistics of the casualties and damage sustained during air raids between 1940-42. A total of 867 bombs was dropped in the area, killing 16 persons and injuring 116 more; 48 houses were completely destroyed, 157 seriously damaged and 3,752 damaged. Apart from this involvement on the 'home front', men and women of Penzance played an active part in the national defence effort; after the cessation of hostilities Penlee House and Park were acquired as a memorial to those killed in action. Penlee House had been built in the 1860s by John R. Branwell, a successful local miller, as his private residence; several times Mayor of the town, he was a relative by marriage of the Brontë sisters. The Park was laid out in playing areas for children, tennis courts and an open air theatre, while the house became a museum, featuring many pictures and exhibits illustrative of the town's history. At the rear of the house are the Chapel of Ease and Garden of Remembrance. The Park, 15 acres in extent, set in the heart of Penzance, will acquire increasing value as the town continues to expand in size and population.

One of the most memorable occurrences of recent years was the great Ash Wednesday storm of 7 March 1962. The morning's high tide brought considerable damage to the Tolcarne, Wherrytown and South Terrace areas; but it was the evening tide, whipped up by an easterly gale, which caused the principal destruction. An hour before high water the seas were coming over both piers at Newlyn harbour, and several boats there broke adrift, but only one was sunk. Loading gear at Penlee Quarry was smashed by giant waves, which also left part of the Newlyn-Mousehole road hanging above a sheer drop, At Mousehole the top coping of the pier was breached, the pier car park washed down to its foundations; all houses facing the sea were damaged and the doors of the lifeboat house swept away. Tolcarne Inn was undermined and the sea wall there destroyed. The Bedford Bolitho Gardens were also demolished, while Wherrytown suffered extensive flooding, people living there, like many at Newlyn, having to be evacuated.

Severe damage occurred all along the Promenade. Water – not spray – was hurled right over the Queen's and other hotels, railings and lamp standards were battered down, and huge holes torn in the surface of the roadway, where the sea ripped out large sections of the sea wall. In one place the Promenade was cut completely in two. Thirty yards of the Bathing Pool wall were destroyed and huge granite blocks washed off the Extension Pier. Nearly four feet of water covered the tracks in the railway station and waves burst over carriages in the sidings, tilting some of them over. Yet, despite all the damage and the flooded homes, not a single life was lost.

This disaster, the worst of its kind since the 1880 storm, brought permanent changes to the appearance of Penzance sea front. The Promenade was reconstructed with an outward curving top to the sea wall, to throw back the waves, and a low wall built along the pavement to prevent floodwater surging along the roadway. But the greatest alteration was to be seen at Wherrytown.

The district takes its name from the old Wherry Mine, sunk in a reef of rocks off the beach, and worked by a steam engine on shore by means of flat rods carried to the shaft along the side of a wooden bridge. Prior to the erection of the mine buildings in 1836 there were sandy towans here and a ropewalk. A few cumbersome bathing machines, drawn up and down by a pony, were kept on the beach between the Promenade and Larrigan River. These were reserved for men, the ladies' machines being located near the 'double steps' and hauled up and down the sea wall according to the state of tide.

After the mine closed in 1838 materials from its engine house were used in the construction of a small terrace called Boase's Row, while the old account house eventually became home to the local Coastguard Commander, later converted into the Cosy Café. In 1883 Norton's Baths on the Western Promenade were removed and new public baths erected in 1887; this building in due course became the Café Marina. In 1854 a large Serpentine Works was erected at Wherrytown to manufacture ornaments and other articles from this attractive stone, quarried at the Lizard. The building, after serving other uses, was demolished to make way for the Bedford Bolitho Gardens in 1916.

The tremendous damage sustained by these gardens, and by houses and other properties in the vicinity, during the 1962 storm, resulted in the redevelopment of the Wherrytown area with flats, shops and a car park, much of the highly individual character of what had once been almost a self-contained community being unfortunately lost in the process.

On 1 April 1974 Penzance, in common with other long established boroughs throughout the country, suffered the traumatic experience of losing its cherished independent status and of being united with neighbouring communities under a new, enlarged local authority – in this case, the Penwith District Council. Its partners in this merger were the former Borough of St Ives, St Just Urban District Council and West Penwith Rural District Council. At St Ives, a new Town Council, with a Town Mayor, was established to serve as a focus for local opinion and to maintain valued civic traditions and ceremonies, while Town Mayors and Parish Councils were allocated to St Just, Hayle and Marazion. At Penzance, a body known as the Penzance Charter Trustees, together with a Town Mayor, was set up, having custody of the ancient charters and regalia of the old borough. A general feeling prevailed, however, that this arrangement was not appropriate to a town of this size and importance, and in 1980 a new Town Council was formed to give more effective representation to the particular views and interests of Penzance. By this means the town may hope to preserve its historic identity, while at the same time participating in the larger aim of creating a more prosperous and efficiently administered West Cornwall.

On 28 November 1980 H M Queen Elizabeth II paid a memorable visit to Penzance and West Cornwall. Accompanied by HRH the Duke of Edinburgh she arrived by Royal train at the railway station, being joined there by Prince Andrew from the Royal Naval Air Station at Culdrose. After unveiling a plaque to commemorate the centenary of the station rebuilding, the Queen drove through the main streets of Penzance, lined by enthusiastic crowds, to Newlyn. The Royal party then drove to Pendeen, where the Queen descended Geevor mine to a depth of 1,500 feet below the sea bed, unveiled a plaque on the new sub-incline extension of the Victory shaft and peered into the old Levant workings to which it gives access. She next visited the highly dramatic coastline at Botallack to view Allen's shaft, Boscawen Diagonal shaft and the Crowns engine houses which had been visited in July 1865 by the Prince of Wales (Edward VII) and Princess Alexandra. After a tour of St Just, she drove through Hayle and concluded her tour with a visit to the Camborne School of Mines.

Procession passing down Market Jew Street during the Peace Day celebrations, 1919. (RCL)

ABOVE: Market Jew Street. (CRO) BELOW: Sunshine on the Promenade. (CRO)

ABOVE: Repairing the Promenade. Note the sand beach, the Battery, Battery Square and Batten's Wharf. Newlyn boats dried their nets here. (RIC/G) BELOW: Penzance Promenade. (CRO/FF) OPPOSITE ABOVE: Sea front near Battery Rocks. Russian cannon and Coastguard Station left, the *Rookery* or Battery Square right. (RIC) CENTRE: Russell's blacksmith's at entrance to Battery Square leading to the Battery Rocks; demolished with the *Rookery* in Battery Square and the old Bethel Chapel for St Anthony's Gardens. (RIC) BELOW: The Wherry mine.

ABOVE and CENTRE: The Wherry mine. (RIC) BELOW: The Promenade Baths. (PHM/G)

ABOVE: Saundry, printer, stationer and bookseller, Chapel Street. (RCL) BELOW: Coulson's Terrace. (RIC/G)

ABOVE: Gun battery above the railway station wall. (PCL/G) CENTRE: St John's Church. (PHM) BELOW: Motorised ice-cream sellers. (PMGL/R)

ABOVE: A fine window display at Bailey & Harvey's. (PMGL/R)
BELOW: Group taken at Penzance Gas Works. (PMGL/R)

ABOVE: Relaying gang, Long Rock, 6 December 1903. BELOW: Building station breakwater. (PMGL/R) OPPOSITE ABOVE: Railway viaduct between Chyandour and Ponsandane. Washed away by several storms it was replaced by a stone embankment in 1921. (PHM) CENTRE: Doubling the line at Ponsandane stone viaduct built in 1921. (PMGL/R) BELOW: Railway viaduct at the Eastern Green. (PHM/G)

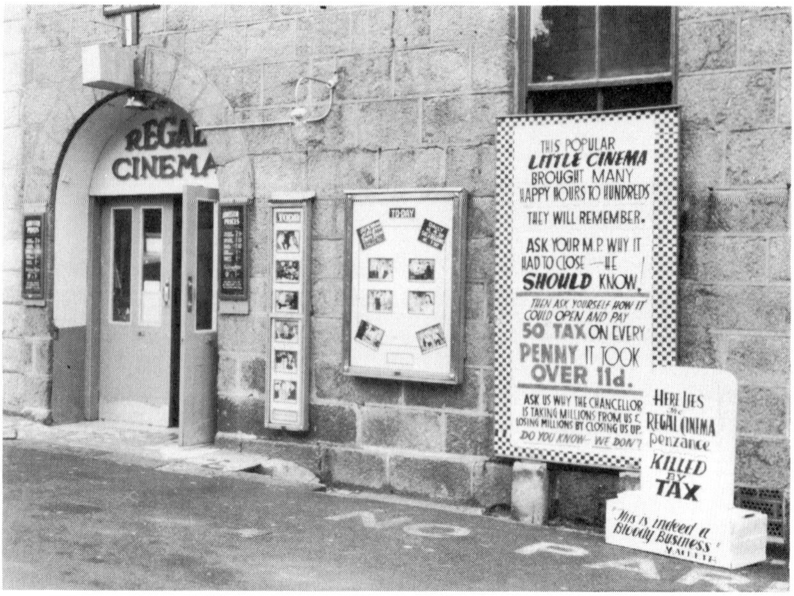

ABOVE: Regal Cinema, victim of taxation, 8 February 1958. Penlowarth Government Offices now occupy its site. (PMGL/R) BELOW: Wesleyan Chapel, Chapel Street. (RCL) OPPOSITE ABOVE: Under Chapel Yard, demolished 1950. (RIC/G) CENTRE: French onion seller at Penzance. (RIC) BELOW: Coinage Hall Street (RIC/G)

ABOVE: Quay Street, August 1912. Probably the oldest street in Penzance. (RCL) BELOW: Public Buildings, St John's Hall. (PCL)

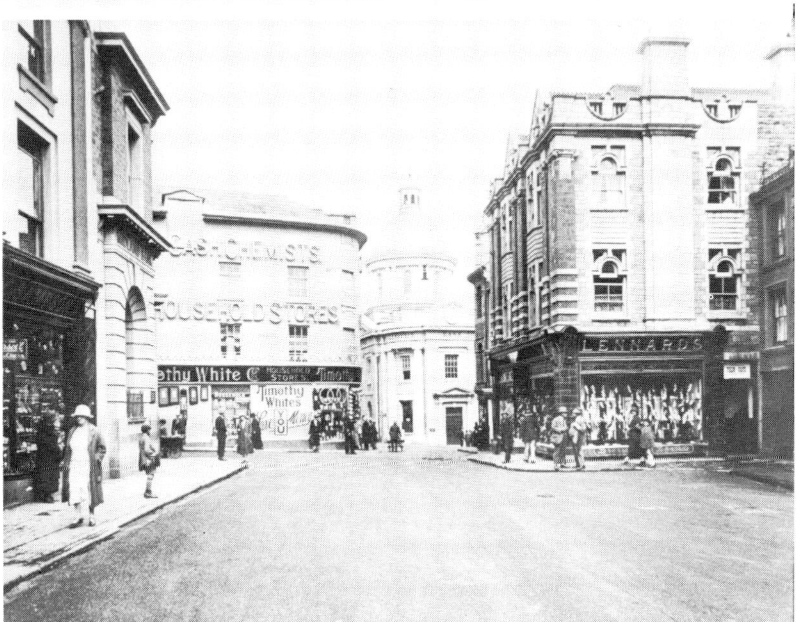

ABOVE: Greenmarket, showing Market Cross and Town Shoot, and BELOW: c1930

ABOVE LEFT: Market Place, from the Greenmarket. Shuttered building (left) was Branwell's grocer's shop, known as the Monkey's Grizzle because of idlers who gathered there and ogled girls. (RIC/G) RIGHT: Greenmarket from the Market Place. Shakerley (chemist) left, Lavin (draper) centre, and Branwell's right. (RIC/G) BELOW: Penzance old town reservoir, Causewayhead. (PHM)

ABOVE LEFT: Keigwin Arms, Mousehole. (RIC/TWJ) RIGHT: First motor 'bus to leave Penzance for London, 30 September 1919. (PHM) BELOW: A group of schoolchildren, Mousehole, 1914. (PMGL/R)

ABOVE: King Edward VII passing the Dolphin Hotel and Docks, 9 April 1902. (PMGL) BELOW: Staff of Simmons, coachbuilder, Penzance. Standing (l to r) William Simmons, smith; John Rowe, smith; Archie James, coach painter; Harry Rich, coach painter; Arthur Rosewall, coach painter; John Farley, body maker; George Berryman, wheelwright. Kneeling, William Allen, coach painter; Hollie Symons, smith. (RIC)

Penzance Corpus Christi Fair: ABOVE: Hancock's Bioscope show, 1902. BELOW: Fair in 1910. (RIC and WMK)

PZ 147

OPPOSITE ABOVE: Effects of the Ash Wednesday storm, 1962. (PMGL/R) CENTRE: Grahame-White and his aeroplane at Penzance 1910. (PMGL/R) BELOW: Whales stranded in Mount's Bay, 1911. (PHM) ABOVE: Penzance Borough Police Force. (PMGL/R) BELOW: Sir Clifford Cory, MP, laying the foundation stone of the Salvation Army Citadel 14 June 1912. (PMGL)

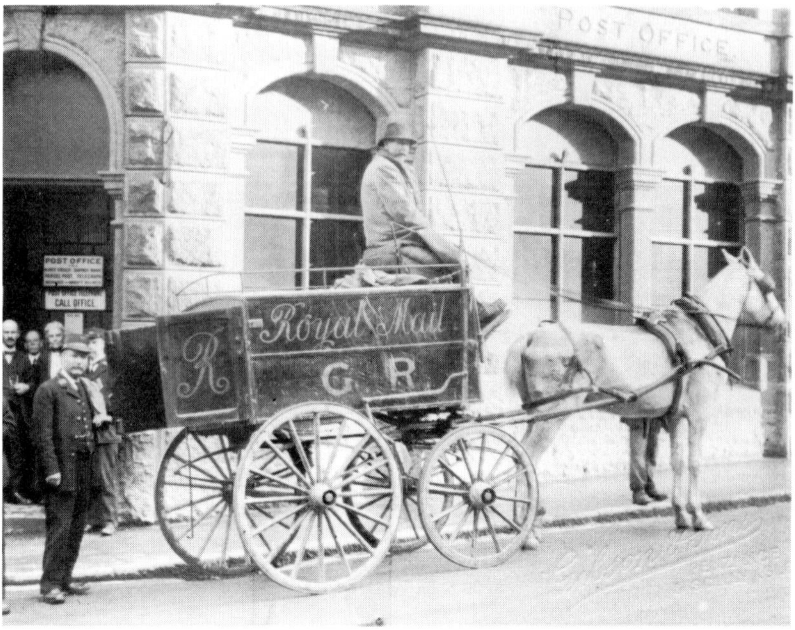

ABOVE: The last horse-drawn vehicle leaving Penzance Post Office for Land's End. (RIC/G) BELOW: Jersey Car setting out for Land's End. (RIC)

ABOVE: Early motor 'bus about to leave Penzance for St Just and Cape Cornwall. (H) BELOW: Triumphal arch erected at Wherrytown to celebrate the end of the '14-'18 war.

. ABOVE: Penzance War Memorial, taken before the construction of the Bathing Pool. (PHM) CENTRE: Penzance cricket team, 1922 (PMGL/R) BELOW: Char-a-banc excursion about to leave the Casino. (PMGL/R)

ABOVE: Rovers Football team, 1922-3 season. (PMGL/R) BELOW: Penzance Bathing Pool c1935. (RCL)

ABOVE: Penzance – St Just 'bus (GWR) with observation car, October 1905. (PHM) BELOW: On the Marazion – Newlyn route via Penzance the steering gave way and the driver, W. P. Bolton, ran the vehicle up the kerb against the Market House wall. (PHM)

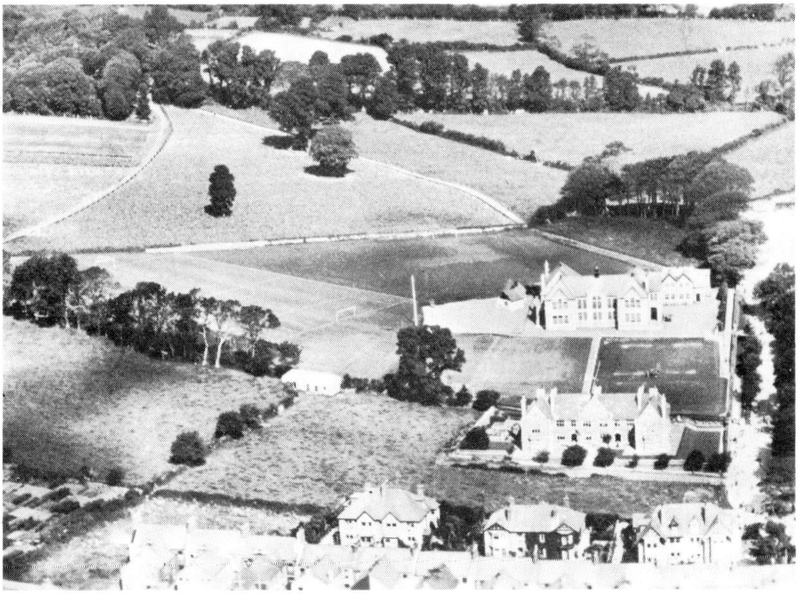

ABOVE: Penzance County Boys' School, October 1932. BELOW: Penzance County School for Boys from the air, c1933. Many of the surrounding fields have since been built over.

ABOVE: Penzance Harbour, 1852. (RCL) BELOW: Penzance from dry dock, May 1857. (RIC)

The Harbour

Penzance harbour, like many others in the Westcountry, owes its origins far more to the fisheries than to trade and commerce. One of the earliest references to the fishing industry there occurs in an 'extent of the manor of Alverton' made in 1327, following the execution of Henry Le Tyes, lord of the manor, for rebellion. There were then 13 boats at 'Pensans' which paid 12d each to the manor, and 16 at 'Mosehole' similarly rated; rents totalling 8s 6d yearly were also exacted in respect of 17 'stalls' (*logiorum*) belonging to foreign fishermen. Commenting on these figures, Canon Doble observed that Mousehole was then the principal centre of population in Penwith, but Penzance was beginning to grow up as a rival to it.

The earliest quay built at Penzance appears to have been the property of the manor, and occupied nearly the same position as the inner part of the present south or lighthouse pier. This quay was already in existence during the early 16th century, as may be inferred from a grant made by Henry VIII as lord of the manor on 16 March 1512 'To our Styward, Receyvour, Auditor, Reves and Bayliffs of our towne of Pensans' of profits arising from the 'ankerrage, kylage and busselage' of all ships using the harbour 'so long as they do well and competentlye repayr and maynteyn the said kaye and bulwarks'. Penzance had thus by that time developed from a small fishing village into a trading port, 'a place of ships and merchandise', possessing both a quay and the means of defending it. Tradition says that tobacco was first smoked in England upon Penzance pier, the presumption being that Sir Walter Raleigh landed here on his return from the newly established colony of Virginia.

The 1614 charter of James I confirmed the harbour rights granted in 1512. In the following year the new Corporation, with commendable foresight, purchased from Richard Daniell, lord of the manor of Alverton, the stone quay and its associated revenues, with other rights, for the paltry sum of £34 and a perpetual annuity of £1 – a bargain if ever there was one. The harbour revenue constituted, with other profits arising from the markets and fairs, the Corporation's principal source of income for many years. The right to collect these dues was farmed out to certain individuals who paid a 'rent' to the Corporation for this privilege. The amount produced by the harbour increased from a modest £21 in 1630 to £38 in 1686, £50 in 1724, £100 in 1746, £126 in 1747, £155 in 1765, £265 in 1786, and £746 in 1806. It was during that year that the standing toast of the Corporation, on letting the market and quay tolls,

'May the market and pier
Bring One Thousand a year'

was fulfilled, the markets being then let for £376, bringing the total to £1,122.

The earliest foreign export from Penzance consisted of smoked pilchards, destined for the Mediterranean, a trade which began in mediaeval times, and continued on a large scale until it tailed off in the late 19th century. This was balanced by imports of French salt, used in the later drysalting process for curing the fish, wine, timber, fruit and other general merchandise. A new export trade – in tin – developed, following the grant of the Coinage Charter in 1663. As the West Cornwall mines were deepened during the following centuries, shipments of this metal, and of copper ore, greatly increased. Down to about 1830 one of the great sights in Chapel Street was the daily arrival of droves of 70 or 80 pack mules from St Just, laden with red-stained sacks of copper ore. Each mule bore a strongly made pack saddle on which were placed two sacks of ore. The animals took possession of the pavements as well as the roadway, and pedestrians were obliged to stand aside to let them pass. Coal was carried on the return journey for the pumping engines of the mines. Carts and waggons eventually replaced the mules, and this traffic so increased that, in 1844, the constricted bridge at Newbridge would no longer accommodate it, and had to be rebuilt by public subscription, the mines contributing liberally to the fund. The waggons gave way in due course to traction engines until lorries finally took over.

In accordance with the terms of Henry VIII's grant the Corporation undertook all measures necessary for repairing the quay, as shown by a few typical excerpts from the Borough Accounts for 1676-7. 'Paid Mr John Tremenheere for the masons and other materialls about the Key, as appeares by his accompts, £25 1s . . . More to the masons about the Key fower Sider hogsheads, £1 4s'. These casks were probably used as lime containers. 'More to them a peice of warpe roape, 16s . . . More to the Seamen for Savinge of Timber washt over the Key head, 1s . . . to the masons Severall times in breade and drinke, 6s'.

An extensive series of improvements to the quay were made during the 18th century. Some of these took place between 1717 and 1719, while details of further work carried out in 1723-4 give a good idea of the appearance of the structure at that period. October 1723: 'To cash payd for bringing up 2 piles from under

Clif, 3s'. 27 January: 'To 565 bush. of lime ashes delivere'd ye Key at sundry times as pr. p.ticulers at 4d. per bush., £9 8s. 4d. . . . To cash pd. Thos. Thomas als. (alias) Dadda for carrying ye same and Clay as pr. receipt, £1 15s. . . . To cash pd. Thomas and William James for carrying of Clay coales and ashes, 8s. . . . To 7 Oak piles for ye Key, £7 6s. . . . To 6 Do., £4 19s. . . . To 57 foot Do. for fillers at 12d. per foot, £2 17s. . . . To cash pd. the Porters for carrying down ye piles and timber at sundry times, 12s. 6d . . . To expences on ye Carpenters abt. ye Key, 6s. 6d. . . . To expences on ye Carpenters abt. ye Key, 6s. 6d. . . . To 383 foot of 3 Inch Oak plank for lineing ye piles and ye necessary ho. at 6d. foot, £8 11s. 6d.' Alas, all this good work was soon to be set at naught by the power of the sea: 11 April: 'To brandy and beer to ye men when y Peer was wash'd down, 12s. . . . To 114 men at several times abt. the Key as pr. p.ticulers at 9d. per diem, £4 9s. 3d. . . . To cash pd. Fran. Treglawn Richard Martin and partners for building ye wall on ye Key and all other work abt. ye Key, £5 13s. 2d. . . . To Mr Thomas Heeps account for Iron work abt. ye Key, £5 13s. 2d. . . . To Mr Thomas Heeps account for Iron work abt. ye Key, £4 2s. 7d. . . . To 40 Tuns of ballast to fill ye key and to pave the same, £1.' 17 April: 'To 2 ps. of plank binding through ye Key, 1s. 6d. . . . To 2 large Corbells in the Key, 12s.'

In 1745 the quay was rebuilt, the Corporation meeting the cost by selling the advowson of Madron, Morvah and Penzance to John Borlase for £800, having purchased it a few years previously for £487 10s. A further rebuilding took place in 1765-7, the contractor being Thomas Richardson, of Plymouth, who immediately afterwards (1767-70) undertook the construction of Smeaton's Pier at St Ives. Following a lengthening in 1785, it was further extended by 150 feet in 1811-13, and a lighthouse erected on its end in 1817.

Meanwhile, the tin trade had increased to such an extent that a section of the harbour was reserved for ships which so specialised. This was the 'Tinmen's Haul', otherwise Cribbin's Zawn, a narrow opening or cove near the inner end of the quay, which derived its name from the fact that it was the hauling-up or beaching place of these vessels. In the early 1800s the tin was carried to London in three little brigs, the business being operated by Messrs Wood and Cornish in conjunction with the Cornish Copper Company of Hayle. They were the *Prince of Wales*, Capt Treluddra; the *Bassett*, Capt Purchase; and the *Furley*, Capt Tom Hosking. These ships were held in high repute, their masters (it is said) being more highly thought of than admirals in the navy. Their trade was considered so important that during the Napoleonic Wars the *Humber*, hired armed ship, Capt Hill, was assigned to convoy the 'Tinmen' to the Downs. In 1805 it was reported that when not actually performing this duty, the *Humber* constantly engaged the French, and on one occasion drove two enemy privateers on shore on the French coast. An active trade in tin was also maintained with Russia. In May 1804 the *Padstow* of Padstow and the *True Briton* of St Ives loaded tin at Penzance for St Petersburgh, the *True Briton* arriving back at Penzance in August with a cargo of hemp and other goods. An advertisement published in 1816 stated that the smack *Active*, F. Tregurthen, master, would commence taking in goods at Penzance for St Petersburgh on or before 6 April and sail direct for that port 'as soon as possible after the Coinage'.

In 1809 a group of merchants, dissatisfied with the existing means of conveying goods between Penzance and London in vessels touching at Falmouth, where they were often detained a fortnight, resolved at a meeting held on 27 January in the King's Head Inn, Penzance, to establish a 'direct Trade' to London 'in good, handy vessels, suitable to the purpose'. So was born the Penzance Shipping Company which, reorganised in 1815, had by 1839 developed into a fleet of nine ships, six being in the London, two in the Bristol and one in the foreign trade. The company enjoyed a long and successful career, but by the 1860s their vessels *Victoria, Joseph Carne* and *Duke of Cornwall* were facing severe competition from coastal steamers such as the *Clifton*, plying between Bristol and London, and the *Empress Eugenie, Rose* and *Genova*, plying between Liverpool and London, which called at Penzance and other intermediate ports *en route*.

An important facility was added to the harbour in May 1810 when John Mathews, shipbuilder, begged leave 'to inform Merchants, Ship-Masters and others . . . that he has, at a considerable expence, opened and completed in a very eligible situation . . . within the Pier of Penzance . . . a safe and very commodious DRY DOCK, capable of receiving Ships or Vessels from One Hundred to Five Hundred tons burthen . . . N.B., the *Thais*, Capt. Rosewall, is now repairing the damages she lately received in the above Dock'. This dry dock, cut out of the solid rock, occupied nearly the same position as the present Holmans' Dock.

At around this period also, Penzance established itself as the mainland base for the packet service to the Isles of Scilly, a role which was to bring much economic advantage to the town in later years. One of the early packets, the *Lord Howe*, when bound to Scilly on 27 June 1819, was totally wrecked on the Kennel Reef inside Mousehole Island, the master and crew having gone below to dinner, leaving a boy at the helm! The passengers and most of the cargo were saved by fishing boats. Subsequent packets included the *Cherub* (1825-37) and *Lord Wellington* (1837-42). In the winter of 1841-2, with the Penzance-based *Sylvia* revenue cutter and other vessels endeavouring to maintain the link in atrocious weather conditions, the Post Office advertised for a new ship of not less than 25 tons burthen, to contract for the service; the letter bag had to be delivered at Penzance Post Office at least one hour before the despatch of the London mail, the packet to sail one hour after its arrival, wind and weather permitting. Sailings from Penzance were on Fridays and from Scilly on Tuesdays.

The contract was won bythe *Lionesse*, which ran from 1842-51, and she was followed by the last of the sailing packets, the *Ariadne*, 1851-8. The first steamer, the *Little Western*, which took over in 1858, and a duplicate, the *Earl of Arran*, were both wrecked at Scilly in 1872. Then followed a succession of vessels, some of whose names are still recalled with nostalgia and affection – *Guide, Queen of the Bay, Lady of the Isles, Lyonesse, Deerhound, Peninnis* and, beginning in 1926, a series of three *Scillonians*, briefly supplemented for a few years by the *Queen of the Isles*.

As the 19th century advanced, the shortcomings of the old tidal harbour, exposed to easterly and south-easterly gales, and with limited wharfage, became increasingly apparent. Indeed, ships often preferred not to use it all. In *Old Penzance* (1956) the late Edgar A. Rees mentioned that many small vessels discharged their cargoes of limestone into the sea just west of Larrigan Rocks. At low tide they were left dry, and carts took away the deposited limestone and also received it from the ships' sides. Similarly, vessels with salt, hides and bark for Messrs Bolitho of Chyandour were beached for discharging west of Ponsandane River, where they escaped town dues.

During the 1830s various proposals were made for constructing railways in Cornwall, one of which, floated in November 1836, was styled 'The Truro, Redruth, and Penzance Railway, With a Breakwater at Penlea (*sic*) Point, Mount's Bay'. The breakwater would have extended about three-quarters of a mile seaward in an easterly direction with a lighthouse on its extremity, so making Penzance an important harbour of refuge; but the scheme which, in railway terms, was somewhat premature, failed to attract sufficient financial backing.

A suggestion mooted in 1839 for building an enlarged harbour with a new north pier running off in a southerly direction from Chyandour Cliff, enclosing a floating dock at its landward end adjacent to the present railway station, also proved abortive; but in 1841 a more modest improvement, involving the construction of a new sea wall, was undertaken. Work began on 5 July in the presence of Messrs R. Pearce, J. P. Vibert and R. M. Moyle. According to the local newspapers, the scheme comprised 'a line of wharfage from opposite the Custom House, and extending from the steps near the Harbour-office to the northern corner of the Dock wall, including the inclined plane near the present Quay slip, a flight of steps near the Custom House, and the return heads adjoining the Dock entrance'. A new harbour office was also erected. Messrs Pawley, Rodda and James secured the building contract, the stone being supplied by Messrs Wallace and Berryman.

Later that year the Corporation adopted a revised harbour scheme and, in 1845, with the prospect of a railway more certain, the foundation stone of a new North Pier, running off from a point near the projected station, was laid on 7 July. The town celebrated this event with a magnificent display of civic pomp and pride. A 'Grand Procession', was formed at Alverton and wended its way through Market Jew Street towards Chyandour. The three ton granite block was laid with full Masonic honours by Samuel Pidwell, the Mayor, amid the roar of cannon and deafening cheers from the spectators.

The procession then made its way to Prince's Street, where a new Fish Market, designed by John Matthews, Clerk of Works for the pier, was officially opened. Described as 'a very handsome and unique structure, in the Grecian style of architecture', and remarkable for the cast-iron columns forming its facade, it was demolished in 1964 to make way for a telephone exchange. To mark the start of the pier and opening of the market, a free dinner to the poor and a tea for the wives and daughters of the fishermen were given in the Corn Exchange; after which about fifty couples, preceded by a band of music, led by John N. R. Millett, and the 'Queen' – presumably Sally Berryman, Queen of the Fisherwomen – danced the ancient Cornish Furry down New Street, up Abbey Street, through Voundervoir Lane and Regent Square to the Esplanade, returning by way of the Folly to the Corn Exchange.

It was intended that the new pier should have a length (including the wharf adjoining the railway station) of about 2,000 feet, and the area of water enclosed was 27 acres. To enable floating docks to be constructed at the northern end, a section of the basin wall was built watertight; but this idea was later dropped in favour of a wet dock at the SW corner of the harbour.

In September 1846 the Prince Consort, when making a cruise along the south Cornish coast with Queen Victoria in the Royal yacht *Fairy,* landed on the still incomplete pier, which was then named the Albert Pier in honour of the occasion. On 30 August 1847 the foundation stone of the sea wall at the head of the pier was laid in the presence of Edward Bolitho, Richard Pearce and John Matthews, the structure being finished later that year.

It was at about this time that Penzance began to acquire some repute as a shipbuilding centre. One of the best known yards was established in the harbour at Newton (or New Town) Wharf on a site where, according to Courtney, formerly stood two pretty cottages occupied respectively by Mr Foxell, the Independent minister, and the Misses Kitty and Mary Davy, sisters of Sir Humphry Davy. Here in April 1846 R. Symons launched a 'handsome schooner' called the *Little Briton*, of 100 tons register, coppered to the bends. Rigged and decorated with flags, 'she glided into her native element in beautiful style, amid the cheering of several hundred persons.' The *Little Briton* was intended for the Mediterranean and fruit trade, her commander Capt Benjamin Pentreath. After the launch about thirty gentlemen partook of an excellent supper at the Dolphin Inn on the quay, the shipwrights being similarly entertained there the following evening.

A second shipbuilding yard was operated by Messrs Mathews & Co, owners of the dry dock. A typical example of their excellent vessels was the beautiful schooner launched in October 1840 called the *Zilli* (the Cornish word for eel.) Owned by the Penzance Shipping Company, she admeasured 89 tons, her carrying capacity 115 tons.

During the 1840s fairly regular sailings were made by emigrant ships from Penzance to the New World. An advertisement published in 1847 announced that the 'First Ship' of the summer sailing season, the fine fast-sailing brig *Resolution*, of Penzance, of 500 tons burthen, W. S. Davies, master, would 'leave Penzance Pier on or about the 1st day of April next, wind and weather permitting, and proceed direct for Quebec, with a limited number of Passengers only, having very superior accommodation'.

In 1852 work began on an extension to the South Pier. Unfortunately, during a terrific SW gale on 27 December, all the scaffolding surrounding the works was swept away and thrown by the heavy sea against the wooden railway viaduct on the Eastern Green, which it demolished. The cast iron lighthouse at the end of the extension was erected in 1855. The Elder Brethren of Trinity House leased a site in the harbour adjacent to the dry dock in 1861 for dressing stone used in building the Wolf Rock lighthouse, the present depôt for servicing lighthouses and warning buoys around the Cornish coast being established there around 1867. Another step towards creating the harbour we know today was taken in 1866, with the construction of the Wharf Road in a southerly direction from the railway station. A further improvement to the South Pier was begun on 9 January 1870 with the laying of the main quoin – a stone of over six tons weight – for a new widened section, by the Borough Surveyor, Mr Morris, in the presence of the Mayor, N. B. Downing, and other members of the Corporation.

In 1878 the Penzance Council decided to construct a floating dock at the southern end of the harbour, in which grain vessels could discharge their cargoes. This work was begun without a contractor, the foundation stone being laid in October 1879. Following the collapse of a dam erected to enable deeper foundations to be laid, the works were let to Mr Lang, of Liskeard, contractor for building the St Ives railway, who completed the 3½ acre dock in November 1884. This structure interfered with the private graving dock established by Mr Mathews in 1810, which had to be partially reconstructed. A new road was also built to connect the floating dock with the railway station; this was carried over a swing bridge (the Ross Bridge, named after Charles Campbell Ross, a local banker, MP for St Ives and five times Mayor of Penzance), designed, in addition, though never so used, to give railway access to the South Pier. The section of this road between the bridge and Wharf Road was taken across a viaduct instead of a wall or embankment, to prevent the rebound of waves into the northern part of the harbour, where fishing boats were moored. After a century of use, the swing bridge was replaced by a new structure in 1981 through co-operation between Penwith District Council, Cornwall County Council, Whitehall, and the European Community at a cost of £600,000. Its steel beams were made in Devoran, being cut and shaped by the Cornish family firm of William Visick & Sons. The platform swings 91 feet through 180 degrees to give seagoing vessels a 44 feet access to the dry dock. The opening ceremony was performed on 9 April by David Harris, Euro-MP for Cornwall and Plymouth, after which two vintage cars, a Bentley and a Rolls, were driven across. Just over six months were required for its construction. During the following year a new 31-ton flap-down gate was installed at the floating dock to replace the original pair of gates, which had opened and closed like a door. The new gate, built by Newton Chambers Engineering Ltd of Sheffield, and installed by A. Dawson Ltd, engineers of Luton, cost £290,000, partly met by a grant of £84,000 from the EEC. The opening ceremony was performed on 25 September 1982 by John Greenwood, a representative of the UK office of the European Commission, in the presence, among others, of Arthur Berryman, Chairman of the Penwith District Council.

Around 1903-4 the old Penzance Dry Dock Company went into liquidation, and the dock was purchased by N. Holman & Sons Ltd, a firm of iron founders established at St Just in 1834 by Nicholas Holman. The works, situated in a valley below the town of St Just, comprised a large foundry, hammer mills, boiler works and machine shop. Huge boilers for the pumping engines in the mines were made there, and the firm obtained a high reputation for the quality of its products. Among them were such diverse items as the Gear Rock Beacon, placed by the Trinity Corporation in 1873 on the extremity of a reef running off from the Battery Rocks at Penzance, and the massive iron railings fixed along the Promenade.

in 1896. Holman's also designed and built the first Cornish range or slab, which became a feature of so many homes in the county, while hundreds were exported overseas, largely to meet the needs of expatriate Cornish miners. The Holman make of slab was standardised by Trinity House, and used in all lighthouses in British waters. The company made a 'coal house' for the original Longships lighthouse in 1841, and in 1836 supplied iron work for the Wolf Rock Beacon erected prior to the building of the present lighthouse.

Quite early in the firm's career a branch was established at Penzance and a large agricultural business built up there. This works made the first iron plough ever used in West Cornwall. The foundry was built on the site of Symons' shipbuilding yard near the former gasworks in the harbour, and the sea washed its walls before the Wharf Road and Ross's Bridge were built. Being thus placed right inside the harbour, a good deal of ship repairing work was obtained, and in this way Holman's first became involved in marine engineering. In 1893 the Borough Arms Foundry, established in 1772, with premises at 100 Market Jew Street, was purchased; although the foundry had been discontinued for many years, the machine and fitting shop survived, and formed a valuable addition to the company's resources.

On acquiring the dry dock in 1905, Messrs Holman pursued a policy of gradual but steady improvement of its facilities, and the Wharf Foundry was eventually transferred there. The first vessel to be repaired in the dock under the new management was the wooden schooner *Margaret Murray,* followed by the ss *Vril* and the Scilly packet steamer *Lyonesse*. During the Great War, when Penzance became an auxiliary Naval Base, the firm's offices at the dry dock were commandeered as headquarters for the Naval staff, while the Company's workforce and facilities were diverted into the war effort. Much valuable and sometimes dangerous work was carried out here during those grim years under difficult conditions. Holman's Dry Dock still forms an integral part of the busy harbour scene at Penzance today, where an interesting and sometimes unusual vessel is nearly always to be seen undergoing a refit in this thoroughly modernised and up-to-date establishment.

The only major development in the harbour during recent times was the creation of a large car park in its northern corner by infilling with quarry spoil from Penlee. It would, however, be insulting the memory of Richard Pearce and the other Victorian pioneers who created the present port to describe this new feature as an 'improvement'. One can but hope that the destruction of so large a segment of this noble basin will not in future years be bitterly regretted. The motor car may yet prove merely a transitory phenomenon, whereas the ship has long centuries of service to its credit, and still shows no sign of becoming obsolete.

ABOVE: An early photograph of shipping in Penzance harbour. (PCL/P) CENTRE: The barge here was used for loading stone for the Wolf Rock lighthouse. (PCL) BELOW: Penzance harbour, 1871. (PCL)

ABOVE: Floating dock under construction, (PCL) and BELOW: in 1881. (PCL)

ABOVE: ps *Queen of the Bay* entering the new floating dock at Penzance at the opening on 11 November 1884. BELOW: Sailing ship passing through the Ross swing bridge. (H)

OPPOSITE ABOVE: ss *Lyonesse,* Scilly packet. (CRO) CENTRE: Masts, sails and spars in Penzance harbour. (PCL) BELOW: Harbour scene, Penzance. (PCL) ABOVE: ss *Scillonian* at Penzance. (H) BELOW: Loading barrels at Penzance. (PHM)

ABOVE: Sevenstones lightvessel undergoing refit at Penzance. (DCV) LEFT: Inner harbour and Dolphin tavern. (RIC per WF Ellis) RIGHT: Nicholas Holman, b1777, d1862. (H)

ABOVE: Gates of Penzance floating dock under repair in Holman's dry dock; the Admiralty paid for wear caused by Naval vessels during the Great War. (H) BELOW: King Harry Ferry under repair in Holman's dry dock after being driven ashore at Coverack, January 1951. (H)

ABOVE: Penzance lifeboat *Richard Lewis* putting off to the barque *North Britain* of Southampton 6 December 1868. Eight members of the crew were rescued by the lifeboat which capsized during the service. (PMGL/ILN)
BELOW: The great storm of February 1883. (RIC/G)

ABOVE: The Rookery flooded with sea water during a storm in 1893. (RIC/G) BELOW: Storm damage at Penzance Promenade in 1895. Notice the layers of sand beneath the macadam surface. A double sea wall from Cornwall Terrace to the western end of the Promenade was constructed in 1896. (PHM/G)

ABOVE: The *Henry Harvey* stranded in Mount's Bay, 25 March 1898.
BELOW: Lifeboat *Elizabeth and Blanche* with her crew. (H)

ABOVE: ss *Taycraig* of London, wrecked on the Gear Rock, 27 January 1936. Penlee lifeboat *W & S* saved nine of her crew. (RCL) BELOW: The present Penlee lifeboat *Mabel Alice* in Mount's Bay. (WT)

ABOVE: A model of the Newlyn lugger *The Mystery* that made the historic 12,000 mile voyage to Australia in 1854-5. (HLP) BELOW: Fishing boats in Newlyn harbour. (PCL)

Newlyn

On Newlyn Hill the gorse is bright,
Upon the hedgerows left and right
Song-dizzy birds the Springtime greet.
The bluebells weave a purple sheet,
Primroses star the lane's green night.

Across the bay each moorland height
Glows golden in the evening light,
And dusk walks violet-eyed and sweet
On Newlyn Hill.

From Crosbie Garstin's *On Newlyn Hill*

Newlyn's pride is its harbour. It has been the reason for its continuing success today and its growth over the past 550 years. Now it stands with its reputation as the fourth largest fish-landing port in the British Isles, for the value of the catch. It is the most important in the south west with latest figures showing a total of almost £7 million for the first time in its history.

We have to turn the calendar back to 1435 to find the appeal by the Bishop of Exeter, which helped to put Newlyn 'on the map'. It was 'to all who should contribute towards the repairing and maintaining of a certain quay or jetty at Newlyn, in the Parish of Paul'.

So the busy harbour and port of today was the 'New Pool' then, with its safe haven. This was recognised by William of Worcester in 1478, who stated, when he visited St Michael's Mount, that 'the chief roadstead of the bay for seamen that come this way is called Gwavas Lake'.

With the coming of the railway to Penzance – and thoughts at one time of continuing it to Newlyn – came new markets and the opportunity for expansion. It was planned on a remarkable scale.

Before 1885, the harbour was for all practical purposes non-existent, with the fleet relying for shelter on the headland which afforded no protection from south and south easterly gales. The old quay was dry at low water and could give shelter to only 40 small boats.

The energy of T. B. Bolitho of Trewidden, who made a loan of £10,000 towards the cost, was a principal factor and the engineer was James C. Inglis, who became General Manager and Consulting Engineer of the Great Western Railway Company.

The first contract, begun in June 1885 and completed early in 1887, was the South Pier, which is 707 feet long, 25 feet wide and was founded on rock. The North Pier was carried out under the second contract, begun early in 1888 and completed the same year. It is 1,025 feet long and 40 feet wide, with two parallel walls chained together at intervals of 100 feet and filled in between with rubble. This pier cost £10 6s 10d per foot run, in contrast to the £30 2s 6d of the South Pier.

The third contract was the North Pier extension, imperative to provide complete shelter to the deep water berths. This was begun in 1891 and completed in 1893, with a total length of 890 feet. Later came the building of the fish market and other improvements in this area, with the road on the re-claimed area linking Newlyn and Street-an-Nowan. The official opening of the North pier came on 3 July in 1894.

There were great scenes of jubilation in those times, with crowds thronging the piers for the official celebrations, all triumphal arches, Sunday best, brass bands and flowers. These were the greatest days of Newlyn's history.

Not only were they the prosperous days of fishing, with mackerel and pilchard dominating the scene, but the quarry at Penlee was a great source of employment and finance.

Penlee stone was used in the construction of the strong rooms at the Bank of England and in Waterloo Bridge. Large quantities of granite and blue elvan were exported throughout Britain and Europe for road building, from the era of 'Janner' and the tramway, through the years of constant lorries, to the automatic conveyor system of today. Today, the quarry scene is a quiet one through the economic recession. The 'quarry guns' at noon are seldom heard.

At the turn of the century Newlyn was the first and greatest mackerel port in the country. Some 15,000 cwt of herring were also landed in 1905, and practically the whole pilchard catch was exported, mainly to Italy. The Methodists' prosperity had a lot for which to thank the Catholic trade.

The value of the catches of this century makes fascinating reading. For mackerel it was £80,511 in 1910, and in 1920 rose to an astonishing £208,018: it was not to reach this figure again until 1975. Then mackerel was landed worth £216,317, and this rose to almost £1 million in 1981. The herrings have all disappeared, and pilchards are little better, but the trawl and line fish have pointed the way to success. This was a mere £19,616 in 1910, £268,591 in 1958, but in 1982 rose to £5,221,777.

Much of the credit here is due to the Stevenson family, and their fleet of trawlers, with brothers Bill and Tony Stevenson and sister Jacqueline Webster continuing the tradition. Their father, the late William S. Stevenson received the OBE in the Queen's Birthday Honours List of 1967 after well over a half-century in the fish trade. He saw the business grow from fish-buying to ownership of the biggest privately-owned fleet in the south west.

The rise in the value of shellfish landings to a peak of £362,560 reflects the success of the Harvey family firm, with brothers Ronald, Jack and Gerald Harvey carrying on the work of their father, the late Matthew Harvey, with the development of special storage tanks close to the South quay.

The Queen met members of both these families when Newlyn had its memorable Royal day in November 1980. She unveiled a Cornish slate plaque to mark the official opening of the new Mary Williams Pier, and the completion of the £1.3 million development.

As had happened a century ago there were cheering and flag-waving crowds, many posies were presented by the children, and everyone hugely enjoyed the occasion. A strip of matting was laid the whole length of the fish market shortly before the Queen arrived, and the Royal group was welcomed by the Chairman of the Harbour Commissioners, Charles Le Grice.

Many were presented, including the Commissioners, and two men who had much to do with the planning of the work, Tom Cotton, the retired Harbour Master, and Alfie Thomas, retired Treasurer, who had over 80 years of service between them.

As well as talking to fishermen and harbour staff, the Queen spoke with Penlee lifeboat Coxswain Trevelyan Richards, skipper of the trawler *Excellent*, and to all the members of the crew. Many of these men were to die a year later in the tragedy of the *Solomon Browne*.

Another presented was Andrew Munson, the present Harbour Master and Clerk, who joined the staff in 1969. He is high in his praise for the new quay: 'You just wouldn't have a port here without it, you wouldn't be able to accommodate the boats. If we could afford to, we would extend it now. Probably that will be our next move'.

One amusing moment came while the Queen was being escorted round the live shellfish storage tanks of W. Harvey and Sons. Her Majesty was being shown round by Ronald Harvey, who picked up a crawfish from the tank. As he did so, the crawfish flipped its tail and the Queen took an involuntary step back in case she was in the line of fire! There was an extra passenger when the Royal train left West Cornwall – an 11lb lobster, which the Queen had accepted.

It was the first visit to Newlyn by a reigning monarch since the early 1940s when, during the Second World War, her parents George VI and his Queen visited the port and met service personnel there.

Newlyn harbour today encloses an area of 40 acres and one special feature, close to the lighthouse on the south arm, is the Ordnance Tidal Observatory, from which the datum for all Ordnance maps in the British Isles is determined. The lighthouse has one flash every five seconds and the fog signal is of one blast of four seconds every minute.

Also on this South Quay is the £55,000 slipway built in 1959 – it was extensively modernised in 1983 at a cost of £80,000 and plays an important part in the life of the port, with its facilities for repair and maintenance.

Newlyn's piers each have a stone to mark the important dates. On the Mary Williams Pier are these words: 'This stone was unveiled by Her Majesty the Queen, on 28th November 1980 to mark the opening of this pier'. At the start of the South Pier is this inscription: 'The Foundation stone of this pier was laid by Charles C. Ross Esq. MP 29 June 1885'. But the most startling is on the North Pier – to show what can be done in one day – with the words: 'This stone was laid to commemorate the erection of this pier on the 3rd July 1894 by T. Bedford Bolitho Esq. MP'.

Down the street there was a blooming riot,
Five and twenty girls were waiting there
And the police they couldn't keep them quiet
One and All, Two and All waiting there for me
For me, for me, 'til I come back from sea,
Anybody know a trick or two, it's me, me me!

Those are the words of the *Riot Song* sung by the youngsters during those remarkable days of 1896 in Newlyn, recalled to me a few years before his death by Richard Cattran. He lived near the quay, and could remember seeing the rifles of the soldiers made into 'tripods' where they were on guard duty.

What an astonishing situation! The Army was brought in to keep the peace in the village after the Cornish fishermen rebelled against the 'invaders' who fished on the Sabbath and ruined their markets. There was violence and there was a celebrated trial – but today the harbour can be as busy on a Sunday as a Monday.

Let Mrs Nettie Pender of Mousehole set the scene. At her home, this local historian with her remarkable memory described it to me: 'I was 2½ years old at the time, but I remember vividly the worry of my parents at the time. I didn't know really what it was all about, but I remember the blinds were all pulled down and the door was locked. My uncle came up and told them to lock the door as the policemen were coming round. I know there was a lot of excitement and that they were very worried'.

Her father was one of those many fishermen who had been to Newlyn to take action against their rivals. 'I can remember my mother going up to the back bedroom window, which faces the bay, calling down to my father "William, come up here a minute the devils are coming again". Now she wasn't a profane woman at all, but when she saw the East Countrymen coming in the Spring of the year they sounded the death knell to the fisherpeople. The more I think about them, the anguish, the worry and the provocation of those poor old fisherpeople, I feel sad to think they had so much to go through'.

'I think that was the reason why our young men went out of the villages. They never had enough to live on and they couldn't face it'. The memories lingered on and the late Mrs Pender recalled that her mother 'never bought a bit of meat of a Penzance butcher in her life after this'. For many Lowestoft boats were at Penzance and had the backing of the traders and there were pitched battles between Newlyn and Penzance.

'The Riots' however, couldn't change the progress and march of time. Mr Cattran told me 'It helped partially, because those who didn't want to go to sea to fish on Sundays, put up a Star flag on the mizzen mast and I think there were quite a few. It lasted quite a while but eventually died away.' These were the 'Sunday Keeps' letting everyone know that they kept the Sabbath. But, now, as he remarked 'they fish on Sunday or whenever they think they can catch fish'.

Life was hard enough for the Cornish fishermen without this situation. Mackerel was plentiful, but prices low and seven day fishing did not help the situation. In May 1896 the simmering situation reached boiling point. Messages went to Mousehole, Porthleven and St Ives warning their Cornish colleagues not to permit the East Countrymen to land their catches. At Mousehole the baulks were put down and a heavy chain fixed across Newlyn harbour. Fishermen boarded the boats which had come into Newlyn during the night and about 100,000 fish were thrown overboard.

A notice went up by the pier, 'No fish to be landed here today'. For those who interfered there was rough handling. Extra police were called in, magistrates arrived to point out 'the folly of their conduct and advising them to disperse quietly'. One fish buyer had his office dragged from its place by the quay to the beach, were it ended up in pieces. In those days there would be some 200 boats in the East Country Fleet, so the economic challenge was considerable.

Next day, a Tuesday, the situation became more violent and special constables were sworn in. Mr Borlase, the Clerk to the Magistrates, was threatened to be thrown into the harbour when he came to the harbour with Mr T. B. Bolitho MP .

In view of the behaviour of the mob, it was decided by the magistrates to telegraph the authorities at Devonport for 300 troops. The Chief Constable arrived and the action of the Harbour Master, Mr Strick, in going out into the bay, in the steam launch

Merlin to warn the visiting boats, was not appreciated. Up went the notice 'New Harbour Master or no more dues. One and All'.

When boats were seen making for Penzance, some 500 fishermen set off but were met there by the borough police, backed up by volunteers with wooden staves. The Newlyn men were armed with stones and sticks, but the police drew their batons and charged the mob, driving them off. Some of the Newlyn men were seriously hurt, they retreated in disorder and did not attempt to attack again.

The 300 men of the Royal Berkshire Regiment arrived on the Wednesday night with rifles and ammunition. They were met by the dignitaries of the town. They marched to the old Serpentine Works at Wherrytown, which was prepared as a temporary barracks and their arrival caused consternation and indignation among Newlyn folk. Armed with improvised clubs made out of broken fish boxes, the Newlynmen went to Wherrytown, and there had the most serious affray of all, in a battle with Lowestoft and their Penzance allies. The mood was ugly, people were beaten up as the Newlyn folk, in retreat, decided to clear the 'white collared' people out of their town.

This brought the celebrated march to Newlyn by the soldiers. The local men shook their fists in impotent rage, there were hoots and groans from the mob, but the police cleared the North pier with help from the Army, the chains were removed, the soldiers posted along the quay. The Lowestoft men quickly put to sea! Then the local men made for the South pier; there were some isolated attacks with stones thrown. One man is said to have had his ear cut off by an officer's sword and another was slightly wounded by a soldier's bayonet. Feelings ran high, but the display of force was too much for the rioters. When the gunboat arrived in the bay, the picture was complete.

As a young schoolboy I was one of the local models for Stanhope Forbes RA, renowned as the father-figure of the 'Newlyn School' of painting. Off I would go, with a young girl companion, to his home and gardens at Faughan, and we can still occasionally find ourselves depicted in one of his scenes. Yet the village had a great attraction for artists in search of the picturesque before the colony began to be formed. It was in 1882 that Walter Langley came from the Midlands and settled there.

'The mild nature of the climate and good light, being favourable to painting in the open air, with the picturesque occupations of the fisher folk, soon attracted artists to the place', he wrote. He was followed by others 'determined to make a place for themselves in the art world', the favourable conditions enabling them to carry on the traditions of the Plain-Air School, then becoming so prominent in France.

'This distinction in their work was soon destined to make a powerful impression on the art of the time in England, when it came to be shown in various exhibitions', added Mr Langley. Soon after 1882 came Mr Forbes, fresh from his studies in France. He painted his first picture of Newlyn life *A Fish Sale on the Beach* which struck a new note when shown at the Royal Academy. Frank Bramley produced here his celebrated picture *A Hopeless Dawn* and Norman Garstin's *Promenade in the Rain* has become nationally popular in recent years. There were many others: Chevalier Tayler, H. S. Tuke, Fred Hall, J. Da-Costa, T. C. Gotch, Mrs Elisabeth Forbes, Edwin Harris, Ralph Todd, H. M. Rheam, F. M. Evans and Harold Harvey.

Newlyn was a busy hive for artists in those years. Some of the earlier members left the village while others came on the scene, including Sherwood Hunter, Mr and Mrs Harold Knight, Lamorna Birch and A. J. Munnings, several of whom made their home in Lamorna. The Art Gallery, built for and presented to the Newlyn artists by the late Passmore Edwards, still provides local artists with a suitable place in which to show their work.

In more recent times the gallery has had fresh vitality and a broader artistic interest, through the South West Arts Council and Director John Halkes.

The village, though, had its other artistic developments, both industrial and decorative. The copper work and the embroidery of the Newlyn Art Industries became well known in the early part of this century for the special character of the designs and craftmanship.

They originated in classes formed in connection with the Home Arts and Industries Association, with the idea of encouraging handicrafts and giving the village boys a chance to earn something for themselves. The class for repoussé copper work soon developed into a self-supporting industry. Newlyn girls had a successful class for embroidery – stencilling combined with needlework – led by Mr and Mrs Reg Dick, and the latter took up the fine art of enamelling on gold and silver, both on articles of jewellery and in the enrichment of silver and copper work. This work is known as the Newlyn Enamel.

That great Breton bishop and missionary, St Pol-de-Leon, probably did much to convert the Western side of Mount's Bay to Christianity and establish a church here. This was the view of former Vicar of St Peter's, Rev W. S. Lach-Szyrma. Paul Church bears the Saint's name, but the Feast celebrations are today hardly even a shadow of their former glory.

In early years there was a chapel at Newlyn, with tradition pointing to Trewavas Street as its site. It was not until 1848 that a new parish was cut out of Madron and Paul, with the first Vicar as Rev George Edmund Carwithen, of Jesus College, Cambridge.

The first temporary church was the building called the Reading Room in Newlyn town, the parish church of St Peter's being erected in 1866 during the incumbency of Rev John Pope Vibert, a Penzance man by birth. The Vicarage was built in 1877, the 'iron schoolhouse' in 1881, and the northern aisle added to the church itself in 1886.

In the church in 1884 was put up a reredos in terra-cotta, representing the Last Supper, after the Leonardo da Vinci painting. In more recent times the work of sculptor and artist, Rev Alan Wyon brought great beauty to the church, with his 'Madonna and Child' in marble, in a recess in the Chancel, and the 'Crucifix' which hangs beneath the canopy at the East end of the church.

Rev John Wesley made an impact on Newlyn that continues to this day, with the Trinity and Centenary Methodist churches. He also, through his *Journals,* presented a record of life here in the latter half of the 18th century. He preached his first sermon at Newlyn in 1747, and made his 14th and last visit when he was an old man of 86. Then, on the morning of 21 August 1789, he preached for the last time at Newlyn at 11 am and, because of the numbers listening was 'obliged to preach abroad'.

Wesley first described it as 'a little town on the south sea,' and walked to rising ground near the shore where there was smooth white sand. It was on this celebrated occasion when some 'poor wretches from Penzance' began to curse and swear, and cause a disturbance, that the Newlyn man Philip Kelynack, 'a bitter opposer till then', declared 'None shall meddle with the man: I will lose my life first'.

A year later he had more problems. He described his congregation as a 'rude, gaping, staring rabble-route, some or other or whom were throwing dirt or stones continually. But before I had done, all were quiet and still; and some looked as if they felt what was spoken'. On future visits he spoke of the need for discipline – and of being disturbed by a vehement shower of rain and hail, as well as being taken ill.

This was a hard-working community, used to poverty, and they took their independence and their Methodism around the world with emigration. At home the Society grew and worshipped in various buildings until the great days of the 1830s.

First came the opening in 1832 of the present Trinity chapel, which has recently celebrated its 150th anniversary. In 1905 the church had 292 members, and the new school hall was built to accommodate 350 Sunday schoolchildren.

In 1835 came the opening of the Ebenezer Chapel in Boase Street, with its cobbled forecourt, and this became the 'old chapel' when the Centenary Church was opened for worship in 1928. The old rivalries between 'Prems' and 'Wesleens' had already eased before Methodist Union in 1932: indeed, Trinity staged a concert in aid of the new chapel up the hill.

Many talented preachers grew up in these: one, Rev Dr William Kelynack became President of the Australasian Conference of the Methodist Church in 1890. Trinity's 150th birthday was marked with a visit by the President of our own Conference in 1982, Rev Dr John A. Newton. Today's Methodist congregations show a dramatic decline from a century ago – but the two chapels are maintained side by side, and still mark 'Street-an-Nowan' from 'Newlyn Town'.

Side by side with the churches, in this century, has been the 'Ship Institute' of the Royal National Mission to Deep Sea Fishermen, linking the fishermen with the faith at the entrance to the North pier. This impressive granite building, of 1911, is very much a part of the port, but before that its forerunner was the Staneley Institute, housed in what was originally a cottage and shop. The work grew so much that through the generosity of Miss Nora Bolitho, the present 'Ship' – so named after its weather vane – was built. At its re-opening in 1969, after extensive modernisation, it was described by the chairman of the Mission Council as 'one of the gems of the Mission'.

The 1850s brought bleak days for the village, which was almost entirely supported by the fishing industry. The drift fishery failed so badly at one time that a committee was formed at Penzance to raise funds towards the relief of distressed fishermen. In 1859 the Board of Trade provided a public barometer for Newlyn's fishermen, set along the cliff near 'Maud's Shop' at the corner of Trewarveneth Street. It was a good omen: the following year brought an excellent mackerel fishery, and in 1861 seven new boats were 'on the stocks' in the village, in various stages of progress. There were other busy industries around the village. The Tolcarne Mill and the surrounding farms spoke for agriculture, and the Trereife smelting house – which dealt with the crushed and dressed tin – for mining. The trade in pilchards for 'Catholic Italy' by sea, and the arrival of the railway at Penzance, brought a tremendous potential for the fishing industry, and led to the need for the new piers. Thc women were as busy as the men in the 19th century fishing industry, the 'ladies of the cowal' as they were described, and even had their own 'Queen'.

> Our Urban council oft we chide
> And rue the day we chose 'em,
> They make in secret dreadful plans
> And see that no one knows 'em.
>
> Our fishermen have learnt but late
> That they must leave the foam
> And daily make the weary walk
> From boat to distant home.

Now shall they shift us up the hill?
Come, let us have a try!
There's many thousand Newlyn men
Should know the reason why.

That was the poem *Our council* that appeared in the Newlyn harbour sports programme of 1937, Coronation Year. It summed up the emotions of the men who were determined that the condemning of so many houses in the heart of the old village – with Gwavas Estate rearing its concrete head on the hill – would not go unchallenged. It reached its climax with the voyage of *The Rosebud* to London carrying local men with a petition.

They were afraid that it would mean 'goodbye to your courts and cottages, your linnhays and lofts and all your romance and charm'. They were right; the planners had struck again. Much of the treasured village that could have been restored or renewed has been ripped out. St Peter's Hill, Navy Inn Court and the Bowjey area have gone. Instead there is Gwavas, restored now to a fine set of homes with massive investment by Penwith Council.

Everyone loves the story of *The Rosebud*, the Newlyn long-liner that went to Westminster in 1937 to save the homes of the fisher folk. It has colour and romance, the spirit of independence and strength of personality to still thrill us. This was surely Cornwall's first battle to preserve the environment. Local folk were determined to prevent Penzance Borough Council's housing clearance scheme from destroying the harbour front and back street cottages of the village they loved.

All who went on *The Rosebud* were Methodists, most of them related to one another. One was my grandfather. I can still recall as a six-year-old boy, the emotional, early morning scenes at the pier as the boat set off. They sang *Fight the Good Fight* when they left and were treated as celebrities and characters when they arrived in London. An uncle, Cecil Richards, who later became a distinguished Cornish fishing leader as the Chief Fisheries Officer to the County Council was at the helm and his brother Billy 'Swell' Richards the skipper. They left on 20 October.

They met the Minister of Housing, Sir Kingsley Wood, who had a saffron cake from Looe sent up from Cornwall to cut up for tea when they came with their petition. With such names as 'Sailor Joe' Harvey and 'Billy Bosun' Roberts among them, and many a local preacher, there was no shortage of anecdote and speechmaking. 'I should have been the fisherman and you the diplomat' said Sir Kingsley to one of them. Much of the Newlyn facade, as we know it today, was saved and many of the little houses remain, but I wonder how much this was due to the Government and Town Planning and how much to the war which interrupted everything within the next two years.

The 50 feet *Rosebud* was built on familiar lugger lines of those days, when sail was just giving way to engines, and was one of the first to be built with engines installed. During the war she became HMS *Rosebud* and saw service around the British coast as a patrol vessel with the Royal Navy, returning to peace time fishing after 1945. A change of ownership brought a change of name to the *Cynthia-Yvonne* – today she is no more, a dead hulk.

A plaque on the wall of the 'Ship Institute' at Newlyn commemorates the most astonishing venture by any group of local fishermen. The boat was called *The Mystery* and it really is a mystery why seven men set off, long before the days of engines and automatic steering, navigation aids, and radio links, to take the little lugger 12,000 miles from home.

They sailed into the unknown from Newlyn on a Saturday morning in November 1854 and ended up in Melbourne, Australia, after 116 days with their 16-ton craft. Little wonder that prayers were said in the village chapel, for the men left wives and families behind as they set off to find a new life. Did it begin as a dare, or as a jest? No one really seems to know, but fortunes were being made in the Gold Rush, and times were bad for the fishermen. It is said that Capt Dick Nichols outlined his plan to his shipmates in The Star, and it was very much a family affair, with Thomas Downing of Vine Cottage in The Coombe putting up £200. The boat was prepared, stores were put on board and off they went to doldrums and storms, high winds and heavy seas . . . plus the heat of the Equator. Within two months she was around the Cape of Good Hope, and the Cornish folk in Cape Town rushed down to give her a welcome.

There were storms and frightening moments on that voyage to Melbourne, with an albatross captured, with wings that almost spanned the deck. There was no happy ending. No fortunes were made in the New World, for the pull of home was too strong. Five of the men returned to Newlyn. *The Mystery* was sold for £150 almost immediately after arrival, and the men did not take up fishing in their new land. Many descendants of those magnificent mariners still live in Newlyn – and the exploits of that crew put many of today's long-distance sailors in the shade.

Before 1908 all ice used at Newlyn was imported from Newlyn in sailing ships – natural ice cut from the frozen lakes in blocks, which varied in thickness according to the severity of the winter. Today the ice plant flourishes in the heart of the port, and just along the New Road is the mackerel cannery of the celebrated Shippams of Chichester. At one time most Cornish harbours had their own fish markets, but now the catches are brought from Penzance, St Ives and even Newquay and Falmouth, to boost the Newlyn totals.

The Ash Wednesday storm of 1962, when huge seas rolled over the piers, could not destroy the work of almost a century ago. For the most part the fishing fleet was safe, although many of the harbour's records were lost when stores on the North arm were carried away by the alarming gale. Great damage was done at Tolcarne, but the Inn – its 1717 date on the lintel – still stands secure.

When the Rt Hon Michael Foot came to Penzance in 1977 it was to honour a man who did much to build the foundations of the Labour Party, William Lovett, on the centenary of his death. For it was Lovett, perhaps Newlyn's most distinguished son, who played a great part in the Chartist movement. A tablet outside the Smugglers Hotel on the harbour front, unveiled in 1951 by Judge J. W. Scobell Armstrong, bears these words: 'As a national leader in social reform he suffered imprisonment for advocating liberties which we now enjoy. 1800-1877'. This was to have been unveiled by Mr Foot's father, the Rt Hon Isaac Foot in 1948, but the event was postponed – the slate split when the carving was almost complete.

For almost 100 years this man of humble origin – he also died in poverty – went unsung in his home community. Lovett was born in a cottage where the Centenary chapel now stands. The hymn book and the Bible provided much of his early reading and his strict Methodist upbringing stood him well. He arrived in London, at the age of 21, with 30 shillings in his pocket, and only twice did he return. The first time was in 1840 – by sea – to recuperate after his release from prison, and in 1852 to see his mother before she died.

In 1831, with the Reform Act close, Lovett was called to serve in the Militia but he had his 'No vote No musket' plan. He objected to serving 'on the grounds of not being represented in Parliament and of not having any voice or vote in the election of those who made those laws that compelled me to take up arms to protect the rights and property of others, while my own rights and the only property I had, my labour, were not protected'.

His views on war were summed up in 1844 in this way: 'If war is the only path to civilisation what a mockery it is to preach up the religion of Christ'. He exposed the serious problems of the poor – and was persecuted and prosecuted for his work. Even after the Reform Act only one man out of every seven had the right to vote, and the People's Charter was the result.

When I was a young lad, at school and Sunday School, there was one song that summed up the Rugby pride that went hand in hand with village life and the bitter rivalry with Penzance:

Molly dear Pint of Beer
Woodbine and a match
We all went up St Goulder's Hill
To see a football match
Old Penzancers tried to shore
Newlyn had them on the floor
Are we downhearted – No, no, no!

Who would have thought that within a few years, by the time I was 14 years old, the two 'enemies' would be together as Penzance and Newlyn – The Pirates?

I don't suppose anyone knows when the first rugby match was played at Newlyn, but it was about a century ago. The supporters needed to be tough to face the steep climb to the ground and the players even tougher to cope with the slope of the pitch. The colours were red and white, there were few facilities at the ground – the cows occupied it most of the time – the players walked up carrying their boots. The first great honour came with the winning of the Junior Cup in 1899. After the break during the First World War came regular Cornish players such as Dick Curnow and Nicky Peake. The generations have been spanned with sons of several Newlyn men who have worn the Pirates jersey. Some names of those Newlyn years come readily to memory – Batten, Stafford, Kneebone, Kitchen, Payne, Harvey and Barron.

Tom Cotton and Joe Barron were two leaders towards amalgamation, the local 'war' was settled long before Hitler's war was completed, and on 22 September 1945 came the great day at the Mennaye Field with the opening match against Guy's Hospital. The men of Newlyn talked of little else, and strict efforts were made to make sure the name 'Newlyn' remained in the Club title and that annual meetings were held at Penzance one year and Newlyn the next!

Newlyn made its full contribution with captains, including Ben Batten, Harvey Richards, Rodda Williams, Mike Jenkin, Owen Barnes, Alf Fowler and Roger Pascoe and in providing such leading officials as Cyril Ladner, Ceddie Barnes, Geoff Mabbott, Jack Tonkin and Jack Jenkin. The Pirates even returned to Newlyn recently with the use of the pitch up The Coombe, close to the turning to that St Goulder, of abiding memory.

It has always been a personal conviction of mine that *Under Milk Wood* owes as much to West Cornwall as to Wales. Think of those cottages and those characters in the fishing village – and you could easily be with Dylan Thomas in Mousehole and Newlyn in pre-war days. Thomas, that lyric genius of poetry, knew our district well. It was in July 1937 that he married Caitlin Macnamara – they were introduced at Mousehole by the artist Augustus John – at Penzance Register Office. He wrote about this time after his wedding 'We're moving to a studio in Newlyn, a studio above a fish market and where gulls fly into breakfast'. He was 22 and as he pointed out, 'with no money, no prospect of money, no attendant friends or relatives and in complete happiness'. He was already acknowledged as a brilliant young poet.

When the magnificent new Arun class £350,000 lifeboat *Mabel Alice* came into Newlyn harbour in May 1983, and was moored alongside the new pier, a link was restored between the port and the RNLI that had been severed exactly 70 years before. From 1908-13 the *Elizabeth and Blanche* was stationed under The Cliff, with brothers Alfred and Tom Vingoe as coxswains. There was no boathouse and it was a 'stopgap' before the building of the slipway at Mousehole. It was a significant period, though, for in December 1911 there took place the last big sailing ship rescue in Mount's Bay, with the lifeboatmen rowing to the ship in distress. There were cheering crowds and a band playing when the lifeboat returned after rescuing the entire crew of 13 of the barque *Saluto.*

Four of the lifeboat's oars were broken in this drama, with the men taken off when the *Saluto* was just a half-mile from the Grebe Rocks off Perranuthnoe. The ship was a total loss, and the only real surprise here was that no medals were awarded. Many other seamen were rescued during these few years at Newlyn, including 27 from the ss *Cragoswald* in 1911, and 20 from the *Clan McPherson* three years earlier. The full circle came in July 1983 with the naming of the new boat by the president of the RNLI, the Duke of Kent, at Newlyn. The 52-ft *Mabel Alice,* with her coxswain Ken Thomas and crew, and the Penlee branch officers and workers, continue the great tradition of service.

Newlyn 1871. (PCL)

ABOVE: Laying foundation stone Newlyn pier 1884. (PHM) BELOW: Newlyn North Pier, 15 July 1886.

ABOVE: Gala day! Sunday school parade on Whit Monday on their way to Trereife for the sports and stalls, the 'treat buns' . . . BELOW: Vine Cottage, one of the most picturesque corners of Newlyn.

ABOVE: Fishing boats in Newlyn harbour c1884. (RIC) BELOW: From 1903-13 the lifeboat *Elizabeth and Blanche* was stationed under The Cliff at Newlyn, in the days when the lifeboatmen rowed to the rescue.

Newlyn scenes; ABOVE LEFT: Old mill. (RIC/TWJ) RIGHT: Duke Street c1900. (RCL) BELOW: Artists' studios (RIC/TWJ)

ABOVE: Church Street, Newlyn, site of the present Centenary Methodist Church. (RIC/TWS) BELOW: A treasured memory 'Outlong' at Newlyn, the balcony scene long since lost for ever.

ABOVE LEFT: Street scene, Newlyn. (RIC) RIGHT: William Stevenson OBE, a leading personality in the revival of Newlyn as a major fishing port. (JHB) BELOW: Newlyn fish market, 1906. (PHM/FF)

ABOVE: Newlyn River and BELOW: harbour.

ABOVE: St Peter's Church, Newlyn. (PCL) CENTRE: Tolcarne. (PCL)
BELOW: Fishing luggers off Newlyn harbour. (RIC)

ABOVE: Laying the foundation stone in 1927 for the Newlyn Centenary Methodist Church. The ceremony was carried out by the Rt Hon Walter Runciman. BELOW: Newlyn Rugby Club in the 1911-12 season with the trophy as junior champions.

ABOVE: On board *Rosebud*. Cecil Richards shows the petition for the Minister of Housing to Alec Beechman , St Ives MP . (SB) BELOW: Pre-war Newlyn Harbour; Lowestoft boats join local fleet. OPPOSITE ABOVE: Street party in the area between Charles Street and Carn Road at the end of the 1939-45 war. CENTRE: King George VI and Queen Elizabeth at Newlyn in 1940s, to meet service personnel. BELOW: Newlyn Male Choir with the Cornwall Championship trophy won in 1983. (AB)

RY CLUB OF

ABOVE: November 1980: Queen opens pier; here, with chairman of the Harbour Commissioners Charles Le Grice and members of the Penlee lifeboat crew.(SB) BELOW: Staff of the Newlyn Fisheries Exhibition. (PHM) OPPOSITE ABOVE: Newlyn Fisherwomen hard at work with their 'cowels'. BELOW LEFT: Fisherwoman with 'rough towser' skirt and 'cowel' basket. RIGHT: Newlyn fish sellers, Betsy Lanyon and Blanche Courtney, 1880. (PHM)

ABOVE: Fresh pilchards! Donkey and fish seller. BELOW LEFT: A Newlyn fisherman. (FF) RIGHT The Boase Street Fire Brigade. (PMGL)

Marazion

There are two facts about Marazion on which there is now little disagreement. *Ictis* was the name given by the Romans to this oldest town in Britain, linked to St Michael's Mount, and the present name has its origin in its privileged Thursday market. With its reputation first built on tin exports, and then on its religious significance, the right to a market was given by the half-brother of William the Conqueror, and in 1250 the younger son of King John granted three fairs and three markets. These gave it an importance above other local communities, and the Michaelmas Fair, in the Long Barn at Trevenner continued into the present century.

The first market was held at the Mount by the monks, later transferred to the shore, and has a place in the romance of Tristan and Iseult with the hermit Ogrin being sent to buy costly apparel so that Iseult would be suitably dressed for her presentation to the court by King Mark.

As with so many coastal towns, Marazion had to face its share of fire and plunder by invaders. In 1513 it was burned by armed men from 30 French ships of war. Turkish pirates were a menace, and in 1640 they took away 60 men, women and children. Today, as part of the St Ives constituency, it shares a Member of Parliament, but in the reign of Henry II it sent two members to Westminster.

Years before Penzance (1614) and St Ives (1639) gained their Charter and borough status, Marazion achieved this distinction. It was granted a Charter of Incorporation by Elizabeth I in 1595 – and in the reign of Elizabeth II, in 1974, again had a mayor after a gap of almost a century. There has been a chequered story, but never a lack of civic pride. The original charter, in Latin on parchment, is still preserved, and so are many other items of remarkable interest, and a great deal of written record down the years. The 'Charter Mayor' was 'our beloved John Wolcocke' and this family name continues in the town today. The Mayor, eight Aldermen, and 12 'capital inhabitants' governed here for almost 300 years. Then, like so many smaller boroughs, it lost control. It ceased to be a corporate town (Municipal Corporation Act of 1883) after 29 September 1886. It became a parish in 1876, as part of the West Penwith rural district, but its priceless regalia, town properties and investments were transferred to the care of the Marazion Town Trust, the first chairman of which was Thomas Lean, who had been the last Mayor in 1886. He held this office on several occasions, and was Town Trust chairman until 1906, when he was 80 years of age. He was also the first Parish Council chairman, with Chris Johnson the last in 1973, and then the first new Town Mayor as local government reorganisation again arrived, and West Penwith became part of the Penwith District Council.

Down the centuries many family names are listed in the leading offices, several of them traders in tin and corn, and including Michell and Field, Congdon, Blewett, Millett, Macpraed, and Hosking. Richard Phillips was chairman of the Trust from 1909-21, and the tradition continues of a Town Trust and Town Council, with separate identities, but there are plans to have the Mayor to serve officially as chairman of the other group.

There has always been rivalry between Penzance and Marazion, but never was it as powerful as in the 17th century. Disputes went ahead with the 'village' of Penzance about a Saturday market – Marazion claiming that an illegal market was an attempt to deprive them of their ancient privileges. They had some revenge when a Royalist insurrection at Penzance was suppressed by Col Robert Bennett and his men from the Mount, with the town pillaged and 40 prisoners taken.

The development of Penzance as a trading centre, as the commercial hub of the Lands End peninsula and West Cornwall, led to Marazion's decline in importance as a shelter for shipping, and as the heart of local markets and fairs. The population of Penzance swiftly outstripped its rival, and now the town has 20,000 to Marazion's 1,600.

The phrase is still used locally, 'like the Mayor of Market Jew – standing in his own light', and this had its origin from one of his three privileges. For in the church the Mayor's seat was in the singing gallery in front of a window. This 'proverb' was expanded and it was later alleged that he had two other rights. He was entitled to sit down to dinner with a parson, and if he was walking in the street and saw a pig lying in the gutter, he could drive it away and lie down there himself. The carved and painted coat of arms in the Town Hall was removed from this old 'chapel' – it was over the Mayor's seat – when it was demolished.

In the old days the Mayor had great powers, from fining people for not going to church, or failing to keep the peace, and could examine the weights of local shopkeepers. There was considerable income from trade, and it was an offence to allow a vagrant or pauper to live in the Borough without asking his consent. The records of his spending included 7s in 1688 'proclaiming ye King', 2s 6d in 1702 for the Coronation, and 5s for a similar event in 1728. Inflation was such, or the celebrations so impressive, that in 1820 the expenses for beer, music and bonfires rose to £3 15s 6d. Back in 1667, 6d was paid to an Irish woman for cleaning the town's stock – near the Town Hall – and in 1823 Daniel Bryant received 18s 8d for 14 days' work, opening the walk close to the church, so important for 'walking' weddings and funerals in those times.

A delightful feature of civic life which is still maintained is the use of the town regalia. The macebearers' costumes are well over 150 years old, with black and silver cocked hats and capes. Among the great treasures are maces, two smaller ones, well used and roughly treated in carrying out their work, and the ceremonial pair acquired in 1768. In those days there was no chain of office, but the Mayor (and now Town Trust chairman) had a malacca cane as a wand of office, given by Francis St Aubyn in 1684 when he was chief citizen. Also of special interest are the two seals, one cut in ivory, and the other sunk in copper. The small maces are of iron, coated with silver and have inscribed in two circles, surrounding a Tudor rose, 'Iohn Asie, Mayor of the Towne and Borough of Marcasiwe, Anno Domini'. The date is illegible but, as John Asye is named as the second burgess in the Charter, it was probably soon after 1595. The 'new' maces are of silver, and in addition to the Town Arms of three castellated towers embossed on the coronal, have the names of the Mayor, Humphrey Cole, eight burgesses and nine capital inhabitants engraved on the shafts.

The two more ancient of the fairs, Mid-Lent and Michaelmas, were still of some importance for cattle, clothing and various other articles until well on in the 1800s and continued to be held at Long Barn, near the ancient grange of the Priors, at Trevennor. The two other Corporation fairs were held at the bottom part of the town, which was the centre of commerce for West Cornwall for probably a thousand years, until the early years of the 1800s.

Although the reason for the fairs no longer prevailed, the custom continued until early this present century when Marazion was visited on Good Friday and there were stalls – at the bottom of the town – the old Mart.

In the past 150 years the pattern of life has changed more than in the preceding seven or eight hundred years. Until the mid-1800s needs were provided for within the town, and a list of occupations included carpenter, glazier, brazier, roper, mason, tinman, tallow chandler, saddler, shoemaker, cordwainer, tailor, cooper, mercer, wheelwright. There was a town bakehouse and a malt-house. Butchers and shoemakers were housed in the Old Market House, beneath the Guildhall, and continued to carry on their trades in the new Market House in 1870. There were also agricultural workers, gardeners, fishermen, mariners, the doctor, solicitor, barrister.

Early Christians at Marazion worshipped at the Mount, and later at their parish church of St Hilary, but in the 14th century the town had its own chapel of ease. This old church, dedicated to St Hermes, was licensed by Bishop Stafford of Exeter in 1397 for divine service. With the destruction of St Hilary church by fire in 1853, and the poor state of Marazion's church – well illustated at the time – there was a call for action.

An appeal was launched in 1857, when the town had a population of 1,300, 'with few exceptions of the poor class' of miners, labourers and fishermen. The need was great: 'The exterior of the building is deplorably mean and unseemly. The interior incurably damp and unwholesome, the floor being many feet below the level of the adjoining street. From its great age and neglect of past generations it has fallen into a state of hopeless decay. The walls and roof are so weak and rotten as to make any attempt at repairs impossible'. The cost of rebuilding was put at £1,800 – a sum beyond the scanty means of the congregation – but almost half was promised by friends. The perpetual curate at this time was Rev J. Murray, and the present building, which covers the site of the older church, was consecrated on 24 June 1861 with the dedication of All Saints, by the Bishop of Exeter. It was made a separate parish, and the first Vicar was Rev J. F. Lemon.

There are, however, some memorials from the earlier church in the present building. Those to members of the Congdon family – prominent in the life of the town – and to members of the St Aubyn family, have a place. A particularly attractive one is dedicated to the memory of J. Piers St Aubyn, 1815-1895, architect of the present church, who was cousin to the fist Lord St Levan. The Lady altar and statue were given in memory of the Reynolds family, and a plaque marks the contribution to the church by Thomas Reynolds 1892-1975, and his first wife Elizabeth, who died in 1943. The pulpit in wood and marble was given in memory of Sarah Coad, and there is a chest made up from some of the panelling of the original church.

Across the road is the well-cared-for war memorial to the fallen of 1914-18 and 1939-45, with a low rail around it. A feature of this is the metalwork, including six bars of music, and the words 'Abide with Me; Fast falls the Eventide', from one of the most famous of all hymns, written by Rev Henry Francis Lyte, a former Vicar of Marazion (1817-19).

Marazion was to the forefront of John Wesley's attention for things other than preaching – and he often visited the town during his 32 journeys between 1743 and 1789. Indeed Marazion was one of his last calls in the final week of his last tour, having 'promised to preach once more'. In 1781, going through the town from Helston to Penzance, he was told that a large congregation was waiting; 'I stepped out of my chaise and began immediately; and we had a gracious shower. Some were cut to the heart, but more rejoiced with joy unspeakable'.

Five years before this he was inquiring if 'that scandal of Cornwall, the plundering of wrecked vessels, still subsisted', and learned that the Methodists would have nothing to do with it. In the 1740s he had a remarkable clash of views with the forces of 'law and order' in those days when he went to find Rev Thomas Maxfield, one of his lay assistants. Maxfield had been taken by constables and was in danger of being sent by magistrates to serve in the Navy and Land Services because he had 'no lawful calling or sufficient maintenance'. Wesley went to Marazion for the hearing by Justices and Commissioners, and was told about 2 pm that they would be sent for when his business came up. Wesley waited until Maxfield was called at about 9 pm, but when he went in he learned that the 'honourable gentlemen' had gone, and that his friend had been sentenced to go for a soldier. Next day he found that Maxfield had been put in the Penzance borough gaol, a wretched place with little light and ventilation, but plenty of rats.

Over the years Marazion has had many places of worship, but the oldest is the Friends Meeting House, built in the 1680s in Beacon Road, opposite the old cemetery. This ancient house is the oldest public building in the town, and has retained its attraction with its decoration, restoration and enlargement.

The strength of Methodism brought several buildings down the years, and fervent evangelical campaigns – particularly at St Thomas's Hall – including the Ebenezer Methodist Free Church of 1862 and the old 1813 Fore Street Chapel used in latter days as a Sunday School. In 1983 the sturdy granite building of Fore Street Methodist Church celebrated its 90th anniversary. One of the great characters of Cornish religious revival, Billy Bray of Gwennap, came preaching in the fairfield at Trevenner in 1862, attracting 1,000 people. In the 1950s Marazion Methodist Church welcomed the President of the Methodist Conference, Dr Donald Soper, during his Cornish tour.

Marazion's most recent development came in 1982 with the opening of the attractive new 2¾-mile by-pass by the then Town Mayor, and Cornwall county transportation committee chairman, Francis Hosking. It had followed 15 years of sustained pressure and work. The opening of the £3.8 million road has brought happier motoring for tourists, but a quieter business life for Marazion itself.

The town had 10,000 vehicles a day at its summer peak, going through its narrow main road, from coaches to petrol tankers and articulated lorries. Old mineworkings found on the site were among the problems faced by builders Reed and Malik, ranging over a length of 110 yards and up to ten feet below the finished road level: a link between Marazion's past mining industry and its present tourist trade. The opening came almost 20 years after another significant day in Marazion's transport history, the closure of the railway station under the 'Beeching Plan'. For Marazion could for over a century boast its own railway station on the Penzance – Truro line, opened in 1852. Now the 'Old Station House' restaurant combines hospitality with the reproduced sounds of the station stop, and nostalgic calls.

Across the roadway lie the large marshes which for so long helped to provide a natural barrier between the town and Penzance, particularly when the sea came sweeping in. It is reputed to have its own ghost, a 'White Lady' who would leap on a traveller's horse and ride pillion as far as the Red River at Chyandour. It is not known if she has been seen since the invention of the motor car and the discovery of electricity.

The town was the centre of a once-important mining area, with such splendid names as Wheal Prosper, Wheal Crab, Tolvaddon, South Neptune, Wheal Virgin, Gwallon, Prosper United and Trebarvah. There were stream works in and around Marazion marsh, and these ventures were active before the slump of the late 19th century. One report tells of the finding in 1849 of an ancient smelting house near the River, with great quantities of ashes, charcoal and slag, and fragments of a bronze furnace with ancient pottery under 12 feet of sand.

A Council school for girls and infants was built in School Lane in 1905, and a boys' school – of 1857 in memory of Sir Christopher Coles – was closed in the 1920s. All children now attend the same school.

George Blewett, in the 18th century, was a wealthy merchant who rebuilt and greatly enlarged the pier at the Mount. He concentrated here almost the whole commerce of the Penwith Hundreds, and his son John built that splendid property The Rookery in 1775. The oldest shop in the town is in the Square, established by Leonard Millett in 1817.

An important development came in 1660 with the Act establishing a letter or packet post, twice a week, by way of Truro and Penryn to Marazion. A hundred years later came another, this time for road improvement, with its terminus 200 feet to the West of Marazion river and bridge. The turnpike house is still in existence at the higher part of the town, and is now a private house.

A proclamation against riotous tinners was read by the Constable in 1728, with the men resentful of the corn merchants who exported what little corn there was, for higher prices overseas, at a time of great local shortage.

Still a feature of life is Ann Pascoe's annual legacy of ten shillings to buy bread on Christmas Eve for the poor who did not have public charity. The capital money was originally used to repair the Market House, but the interest is still paid each year . . . . . nowadays to the Vicar, for the poor.

'Free' newspapers are nothing new in Marazion! The *Marazion and district Advertiser* began on 1 May 1920, printed by Frederick Worden, but cost a penny when it closed with its issue of 15 August 1942. This last edition told of the war-time 'Tanks for Attack' fund-raising.

The first appointed Clerk of the Borough was Thomas Clutterbuck in 1775, and the last one was Thomas Cornish. The Trust still has an income from property in the town, and owns the Town Hall built in 1870 on the site of an earlier Guild Hall. There are today nine Trustees, five elected by the Town Council, and four co-opted. In 1977, to mark the silver jubilee of the Queen's reign, the Trust presented silver jubilee crowns to the children of the town at a cost of £67.

Marazion 'Apollo' male choir have a special place in the affections of the town. They have earned a reputation among the top choirs of the nation in recent years, and taken some of the principal honours. The choir, with its remarkable record of loyalty as well as success, has done much to set standards for male voice singing throughout the south west. Eighty years of glorious song – and still the honours come. Former chorister John Treleaven is now principal tenor with the English National Opera company. One great moment came in 1969 when they gained under their then musical director John J. Matthews, first prize in the advanced class of England's premier festival, Blackpool. He had taken over the baton in 1950, and the choir blazed a trail that twice took them to the Burma Star Reunion in London's Albert Hall to sing before members of the Royal family, to the championship of the London music festival in 1958 and in the 1970s, and more recently on a tour of the United States. Little wonder they earned the name of Cornwall's Ambassadors of Song. A crowning glory came with their performance at the International Eisteddfod at Llangollen in 1975 when they attained the highest marks of any British choir. Many radio and television appearances have come with success at these and other festivals in Cornwall and 'abroad'. Nicholas Matthews is the new conductor, and his association as singer, accompanist and deputy conductor stems from his youth. The choir had its beginning in 1904, founded by Ted Harris, son of a Methodist Minister. When he left, John Henry Trudgeon took over and did great work for 40 years. He celebrated his 70th birthday with the choir in 1942, retiring in 1945, Tolefree Parr and Leslie Jacobs succeeding him.

ABOVE: The Old Marazion Church probably in the 1840s. BELOW: The fire engine *Lillie* in about 1890. Centre is Thomas Francis Hosking, Captain of the Marazion Fire Brigade.

ABOVE: The Old Market House pictured in 1869. The Town Hall is now on this site. BELOW: Gathering seaweed at Marazion. (CRO/FF)

ABOVE: Beach party, Marazion, 1912 (RCL) and **BELOW: Marazion's** traffic-free Main Street.

ABOVE: Marazion Apollo male voice choir: front row l to r – Chairman Ken Cargeeg, President Peter Tresidder, conductor Nicholas Matthews, accompanist Dennis Bennetts. (TF) BELOW: Marazion Town Council, 1983, Mayor Francis Hosking; back row l to r – Paul Stevens, Rex Laity, Francis Hosking, Stan Crowle, Chris Hales: front – Godfrey Varker, Chris Johnson, Sidney Trembath, Reuben Collins, Jim Rodda. (SB)

ABOVE: Royal yachts lying off the Mount, 5 September, 1846 (PMGL/ILN) and BELOW: St Michael's Mount, 1816. (RCL)

The Mount

By the Orient gleam
Whitening the foam of the blue wave that breaks
Around his granite feet, but dimly seen,
Majestic Michael rises. He whose brow
Is crown'd with castles, and whose rocky sides
Are clad with dusky ivy; he whose base,
Beat by the storm of ages, stands unmoved
Amidst the wreck of things, the change of time.

That base, encircled by the azure waves
Was once with verdure clad: the tow'ring oaks
There waved their branches green – the sacred oaks
Whose awful shades among, the Druids stray'd
To cut the hallow'd mistletoe, and hold
High Converse with their Gods.

These lines, in classical style, were written by that great scientist, Sir Humphry Davy, as part of his poem on Mount's Bay. He loved his local landscape, and this scene of 'Majestic Michael' must have looked much the same to him, almost 200 years ago, when he was a young lad, as it does to us today.

It is so easy to be lyrical about one of the nation's greatest treasures, layered in legend, in religious and military history, so crowded with beauty and grandeur. It is almost 340 years since the St Aubyn family began their distinguished connection when, on 17 June in 1647, Col John St. Aubyn was nominated Captain of the Mount by Parliament.

The St Aubyn tradition continues through the present Lord and Lady St Levan, who make the Mount their home. He succeeded to the title in 1978, on the death of his father.

The family did not always live there. There were celebrations in 1826 when Sir John St Aubyn visited the Mount. The guns on the ramparts were fired, the chapel bells rung, the ancient standard displayed, and a 'sumptious' dinner enjoyed.

The giant Cormoran is reputed to have built the Mount island with granite brought from Castle-an-Dinas by his wife. Chapel Rock, in legend, had its place on the shore of Marazion when he gave her a kick for her laziness, and the greenstone boulder in her apron rolled into the sea!

In the 15th and 16th centuries there was a little Chapel here, used by pilgrims before going onto the causeway that connects Mount and town at low water, but Lord Hopton at the command of Prince Charles, ordered this 'old decayed chapel' to be pulled down.

Myth and mystery abound. There is the 'Giant's Well' where Jack the Giant Killer is reputed to have slain Cormoran, and 'St Michael's Chair' which gives the mastery to the first of a married couple who sit on it. There is only room for one! The collapse of Lanyon Quoit in 1815 was believed to have been caused by people digging there in the hope of discovering the giant of the Mount and his treasure.

One delightful tradition tells of the visit of the boy Jesus to the Mount, brought by Joseph of Arimathea, while trading for tin. Christians have worshipped here for well over a thousand years, pilgrims have come in their tens of thousands, following the tradition of the miraculous apparition of St Michael, the Archangel, at 'the hoar rock in the wood'.

Historians write of Ictis, whence tin was exported to the Mediterranean, long before the birth of Christ. There can be little doubt, from the written and visual evidence, that the Mount once looked out upon a wooded valley and not a bay. The sea came upon the shore, and buried towns and men, oxen and sheep.

No one knows when the monks first settled here, and there is a tradition that St Cadoc and St Keyne visited in the 5th century. The Mount was given by King Edward the Confessor to the Abbey of Mont St Michel in Normandy in the 11th century. The monks at the Cornish priory were of the Order of St Benedict, and an early honour came from Pope Gregory with a papal indulgence of a remission of one third part of penance for pilgrims.

The link with Mont St Michel continued after the Conquest, through Robert, Count of Mortain, half-brother of William the Conqueror. He became the first Earl of Cornwall, and as he had lived a few miles from the 'Mont', the Cornish Mount must have looked like a second home to him.

When Philip II of France invaded Normandy during King John's unworthy reign, the Mount became an 'alien priory' and its status changed. In 1349, after the Black Death had spent its force, John Hardy became the first Prior at the Mount with an English name, and in a 1424 charter of Henry VI it became part of the endowment of the Brigittine Syon Abbey at Isleworth.

In the 15th century, when there were few monks in residence, the leader was described as Archpriest. Among the relics were some of the stones of the sepulchre of Jesus, an arm bone of Saint Felix Martyr. There were three altars in the church at this time, the high altar with its tabernacle, and a box containing the relics, and those of St Michael and the Crucified Saviour.

A new chapter in the life of the Mount – it rises 250 feet above sea level and is then crowned by the Castle – began in August 1425, with first word of an indulgence from the Bishop of Exeter to help with the work of building a breakwater. Merchant ships and fishing boats paid 'quayage'. As the years passed so the church became richer, and the relics then included two pieces of the Cross, but then came the Act of Parliament in 1536, through Henry VIII, for the dissolution of the lesser monasteries. Historian Canon T. Taylor holds to the view that an inventory of the Mount was made the previous year, the valuables sent to London, and the plunder legalised by the Act.

There were a few owners down the century until the Mount came into the possession of Colonel John St Aubyn in 1659. The 3rd Lord St Levan gave it to the National Trust in 1954.

Royalty have visited down the centuries. Prince Charles, later Charles II, is thought to have left from here for the Scillies. Queen Victoria made two visits, her son Edward VII came in 1901, and in more recent years the Queen Mother and Duke of Gloucester have been among the guests. So too has Prime Minister Mrs Margaret Thatcher.

Even the celebrated Pretender, Perkin Warbeck, who fooled half a continent, came to Cornwall from Cork in 1497, landing at Sennen, and entering the Mount without opposition. He left his wife, Lady Catherine Gordon, daughter of the Earl of Huntly there, and went on with his force to Bodmin, issuing a proclamation in the name of Richard IV, and having 6,000 men. A costly setback at Exeter was followed by the desertion of his army at Taunton, and his end came with him being hanged, drawn and quartered. His wife, still at the Mount, was found by the King's cavalry, and she was brought to the King as a prisoner.

There seemed constant drama here. In 1549, Humphry Arundell, who had been appointed Mount Governor by the King, led the Cornish rising against the new English Prayer Book, and was hanged at Tyburn the following January. The Earl of Oxford, John de Vere, a great Lancastrian, went to Dieppe after the victory by the King at the battle of Barnet in 1471, and then came to the Mount. With his many men disguised as pilgrims, the Earl took possession from the end of September until his defeat after a 26-week-long seige . . . but lived to fight again. He returned from France with Henry, Earl of Richmond at the battle of Bosworth, and triumphed when Richard III was slain, and Henry VII acceded to the throne.

Sir Francis Basset, who possessed the Mount in 1640, was on the side of the King when many in Cornwall were for the Parliament . . . and some families were for both. He died a fortnight after the

King had said that he left Cornwall to Basset 'safe and sound'. The Mount was readily recognised as an important fortress.

Col John St Aubyn was the last Governor to maintain a garrison here, the quay was restored by the third Baronet, Sir John, in 1726-27, and around 1750 the Lady Chapel was converted into two drawing rooms. The church was restored to its original use in 1811, and the first Lord St Levan erected the east wing in the 1870s.

In April 1943 Mass was offered at the Mount for the first time since the Reformation, as Canon J. R. Fletcher has pointed out, after one of the rooms was converted into a private oratory. The Dowager Lady St Levan, who has been a devoted enthusiast and worker for the nearby Cheshire Home of St Teresa, is a Roman Catholic.

A few years before this, with the outbreak of the 1939-45 war, soldiers were again stationed on the Mount. A platoon of infantry was based here but, despite bombing at Penzance and Newlyn, there were no bombs dropped on the Mount and there were no casualties when the village was machine-gunned by enemy aircraft.

From a pilgrim's shrine, and a Priory, it became a castle and a fortress. Today it is a home, and the pilgrims come in even larger numbers. They have a hundred languages, dialects and accents but all come in peace. The invasion is by the tourists who marvel at the majesty of the scene as they trek along the granite causeway or enjoy the boat trip. In 1982 there was a total of 165,000 visitors. Lord St Levan is responsible, with the National Trust, for the showing arrangements, and all the income is used to maintain the property. After the audio-visual display, the visitor can climb to the castle showrooms, going through the Armoury and study, the breakfast and Chevy Chase rooms, the terraces and chapel, Blue drawing room, map room, long corridor, Garrison room and Museum. The Mount and its castle is the jewel in the crown of the St Aubyn family and the National Trust.

The Mount boatmen in 18th century livery.

St Michael's Mount. (RCL)

LEFT: Chevy Chase Room, St Michael's Mount (NT) and RIGHT: Lord and Lady St Levan (DW) with BELOW: a schooner in the Bay. (PCL)

St Michael's Mount. **(RW)**

Bibliography

The Hayle, West Cornwall and Helston Railways G. H. Anthony 1968
A Week at the Land's End J. T. Blight 1861
Churches of West Cornwall J. T. Blight 1885
The Antiquities of Cornwall Dr William Borlase 1754
The Natural History of Cornwall Dr William Borlase 1758
Traditions and Hearthside Stories of West Cornwall William Bottrell 1870, 1873, 1880
Statistical Account of the Parish of St Just in Penwith Rev John Buller 1842
The Survey of Cornwall Richard Carew 1769 ed.
Early Tours in Devon and Cornwall R. Pearse Chope 1918
Half a Century of Penzance Louise Courtney 1878
A Guide to Penzance J. S. Courtney 1845
Chronological Memoranda Relating to the Town of Penzance J. S. Courtney 1839
Old Penzance and St Mary's Chapel Canon G. H. Doble no date (This includes valuable notes by C. Henderson and R. M. Nance on the Topography of Penzance.)
Brasses of Cornwall Dunkin
The Land's End District Richard Edmonds 1862
West Country Passenger Steamers Grahame Farr 1967
Historical Survey of the County of Cornwall C. S. Gilbert, 1817
The Parochial History of Cornwall Davies Gilbert 1838
The Archaeology of Cornwall and Scilly H. O'Neill Hencken 1932
The Ecclesiastical Antiquities of the 109 Parishes of West Cornwall Charles Henderson (in the *Journal of the Royal Institution of Cornwall,* 1956, 1958, 1960)
University Extension Lectures given at Penzance in 1924-5 on the History of West Cornwall. Charles Henderson.
Parochial History of Cornwall (in the Cornish Church Guide) Charles Henderson 1925
The Land's End W. H. Hudson 1911
The Story of St Mary the Virgin, Penzance, Canon H. R. Jennings n.d.
Newlyn and its Pier Rev W. S. Lach-Szyrma 1884
A Short History of Penzance, St. Michael's Mount, etc. Rev W. S. Lach-Szyrma 1878
Penzance, Past and Present George Bown Millett 1876

Cornish Seines and Seiners Cyril Noall 1972
Smuggling in Cornwall Cyril Noall, 1971
Wreck and Rescue Round the Cornish Coast Cyril Noall and Grahame Farr Vol. 2, The Land's End Lifeboats, 1965
The Wesleys in Cornwall John Pearce 1974
The Ports and Harbours of Cornwall Richard Pearse 1963
A Guide to the Mount's Bay and the Land's End A Physician (Dr J. Ayrton Paris) 1824
Biographical Sketches in Cornwall R. Polwhele 1831
Old Penzance Edgar A. Rees 1956
The Domesday Survey for Cornwall (in the Victoria County History of Cornwall), L. F. Salzman and Thomas Taylor, 1924
Excursions in the County of Cornwall F. W. L. Stockdale 1824
The Official Guide to Penzance 1876
A Description of England and Wales Vol II, Cornwall, 1769
(The Borough of Penzance), published without title or date, apparently by Penzance Borough Council
The Story of an Old Established Business in West Cornwall: N. Holman & Sons, Ltd., of St. Just and Penzance, 1934
'One and All' Almanac Saundry's 1930
Penzance Views and Reviews: 1898 (reprinted 1975).
Penzance Corporation Records (at the County Record Office, Truro).
Records of St Mary's Church, Penzance (at the County Record Office, Truro)
Journal of the Royal Institution of Cornwall
Old Cornwall Journal
Files of the *Royal Cornwall Gazette, West Briton, Penzance Gazette, Penzance Journal, Cornish Telegraph* and *Cornishman.*
Some Recollections of Old Newlyn Suzanne B. Humphrys
Newlyn Towners, Fishermen and Methodists Ben Batten
Marazion and St Michael's Mount Edna Waters Coward
Short History of St Michael's Mount Canon J. R. Fletcher
Saint Michael's Mount Rev T. Taylor

Index

Key to Caption Credits

AB	Andrew Besley	NT	National Trust
AE	Alfred Eddy	P	Preston
BL	British Library	PCL	Penzance County Library
BM	British Museum	PHM	Penlee House Museum
CH	Rev Charles Hutton	PMGL	Penzance Morrab Gardens Library
CRO	County Record Office, Truro	PRO	Public Record Office
DCV	Douglas Vosper	R	Richards, Penzance
DM	Dick Matthews	RCL	Redruth County Library
DW	David Woods	RIC	Royal Institution of Cornwall
FF	Francis Frith	RW	Roland Woods
G	Gibson	SB	Sam Bennetts
GW	George Waterhouse	TF	Ted Ford
H	Holmans, Penzance	TWJ	T. W. Jones
ILN	*Illustrated London News*	WMH	W. M. Harrison
JB	Jim Bottrell	WMK	W. M. Keating
JJC	J. J. Churchward	WR	Rev William Rowett
NPG	National Portrait Gallery	WT	William Thomas

Subscribers

Presentation copies

1 Penzance Town Council
2 Penwith District Council
3 Marazion Town Council
4 Cornwall County Council
5 Cornwall County Library
6 Lord & Lady St Levan
7 Councillor Mrs Margaret Beckerleg JP
8 Cyril Noall
9 Douglas Williams
10 William Thomas

11 Clive & Carolyn Birch
12 Penlee House Museum
13 Mrs D. Miller
14 M.C. Nicholls
15 Betty Wren
16 D.E. Eastaway
17 Mrs Jean Eady
18 D.R. Blewett
19 Julyan Drew
20 C.R. Roberts
21 P.R. Chivers
22 T.P. French
23 W. Grant
24 D.M. Thomas
25 Cecil Dunn
26 J.A. Taylor
27 Arthur Edgar & Lowella Pearce
28 W.G. Tunmore
29 Mr & Mrs H.S. Saunders
30 Mr & Mrs R.L. Rogers
31 Mrs Diana Waugh
32 Mrs W. Allsop
33 Mrs Barbara Hosking
34 Mrs R.E. Rowe
35 R.D. Angove
36 Robert G. Coles
37 N.E. Osborne
38 Canon Romilly Craze
39 Mrs B.E. Lavens
40 Canon Romilly Craze
41 C.C. Jeffery
42 Mrs Jacqueline Hill
43 Miss Julie Carpenter
44 Mrs Irene Carpenter
45 Ms E. Mumford
46 Mr & Mrs P. Hawksley
47 G. Corrall
48 Mrs L.U. Doyle
49 Mrs Mary Cullen
50 D.W. Berryman
51 Mrs E.M.S. Hitchens
52 Mrs Sylvia Chapman
53 Mrs M. Elizabeth Rodda
54 Mrs J. Newport
55 Mr & Mrs F.M. Jenkin
56 Paul Vibert
57 D.S. White
58 E. Wallis
59 Mrs M. Williams
60 Mr & Mrs H. Lea
61 P.P. Harvey
62 Kenneth Leonard Madkan
63 George Ordish
64 F.S. Holman
65 Aileen F.L. Bridge
66 M. Dorey
67 J.R.A. White
68 Mrs D. Tredinnick
69 J.P. Treglown
70 P.J. Martin
71 Beryl & Andy Spinelli
72 A. Williams
73 Derek G. Reynolds
74 F.J. Peak
75 John Drew
76 Miss M. Moore
77 Michael Rice
78 Richard A. Ross
79 John Hooper
80 J. Eric Hunt FICS
81 Mrs G. Bird
82 J.G. Barton
83 Mr & Mrs R.J. Francis
84
85 Mrs L. Gowers
86 J. H. Adams
87 Lionel Hicks
88
89 Mrs C. Fisher
90 Terry Johns
91 E.J. Johns
92 Julie Dodd
93 Mrs E. Bunn
94 Glyn Jenkins
95 Barclays Bank Ltd, Penzance
96 Dorothy Richards
97 Francis Hosking
98 Basil I. Green
99 Mrs B. Iwanoska
100 Mrs F.P. Watson
101 N.B.J. Huijsman CMG
102 L.H. Roberson
103
104 Major S.E. Bolitho MC
105 J.F. Purchas
106 P.A. Hughes
107 Morwenna Veal
108 Andrew C.V. Hawke
109 Betty Hill
110 Canon J.H. Adams
111 Vivian Rowe
112 Cornwall County Record Office
113 Mrs Pam Astrinsky
114
115 Penwith Sixth Form College
116 J.P. Treglown MPS ARPS
117
118 W.W. Cock
119 Lescudjack CS School, Penzance
120 W.E. Leak
121 David & Sonia Daniel
122
124 Cyril Noall
125 Mrs E.M. Mitchell-Fox
126 Brian J. Coombes
127 W.J.E. Elvy
128 Justin Brooke
129 John Hodges
130 Sydney E. Ward
131 Mounts Bay School, Penzance
132 Mrs A.N. Larkworthy
133 Richard Perkin
134 John Blowey

135 Bruce Burley
136 Mrs Sylvia Chapman
137 R.K. Cocks
138 S.C. Field
139 Professor Charles Thomas
140 Mrs M. Worledote
141 G.M. Palmer
142 S.E. Ward
143 R.L. Bowley
144 D.J.G. Corin
145 C.J. Davies
146 M.E. Price
147 Arthur Charles Cutter
148 Miss M. Bradby
149 B.R. Allen
150 Mr & Mrs M.E. Greenhalgh
151 Cornwall County Record Office
152 John Francis Purchas
153 Godfrey Adams
154 Justin Brooke
155 John Hodges
156 F.T. Hosking
157 Mrs Sylvia Lee
158 B.M. Kirk
159 H. Penna
160 O.C. Collier
161 Falmouth School
162 M.J.H. Tonking
163 Sir James Smith's School, Camelford
164 Mr & Mrs R. S. Pope
165 Leonard Hosking Truran
166 R.C. Langley
167 Capt R.T Williams
168 Mrs F.R. Reardon
169 Dr R.J. Hetherington
170 Godfrey Adams
171 Mrs N. Berryman
172 D.G. Berryman
173 Victoria & Albert Museum
174–208 Cornwall County Library
209 Mr & Mrs W. Thomas
210 Mrs D.M. Bailey
211 Nigel E. Nethersole
212 M. Greenhalgh
213 B. Mitchell
214 E. Phillips
215–216 Miss L. Clark
217 Miss M.W. Polsue
218 W.T. Bennetts
219 S.W. Cocking
220 I. Woolcock
221 Mrs L.M. Prior
222 Mr & Mrs S.W. Peters
223 Peter B. Evans
224 Mr & Mrs R. Tugwell
225 Sonia & David Daniel
226 Charles Bray

Remaining Names Unlisted:

End papers Ordnance Survey map of Penzance.

Spring
Municipal Boundary
Rosevean House
Penare House
Medrose Cottage
Leskinnick House
Spring
Richmond Villa
Richmond House
E A S T   W A R D
R.C. Chapel
Dispensary & Infirmary
School (Boys & Girls)
Bible Christian Chapel
Rope Walk
School (Boys, Girls & Infants)
TAROVEOR ROAD
CATTLE MART
Clarence House
St. Paul's Church
Penalverne House
BELGRAVIA STREET
Friends Meeting House
P E N Z A N C E